Saudi Arabia

Saudi Arabia

BY ANN HEINRICHS

Enchantment of the World
Second Series

Children's Press®

A Division of Scholastic Inc.

NEW YORK TORONTO LONDON AUCKLAND SYDNEY
MEXICO CITY NEW DELHI HONG KONG

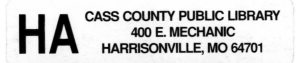

Frontispiece: Medina's Qoba mosque at dawn

Consultant: Amy J. Johnson, Assistant Professor of History, Berry College, Mount Berry, Georgia

Please note: All statistics are as up-to-date as possible at the time of publication.

Book production by Herman Adler Design

Library of Congress Cataloging-in-Publication Data

Heinrichs, Ann.
      Saudi Arabia / by Ann Heinrichs.
      p. cm. — (Enchantment of the world. Second series)
      Includes bibliographical references and index.
      ISBN 0-516-22287-2
      1. Saudi Arabia—Juvenile literature. [1. Saudi Arabia.] I. Title. II. Series.
DS204.25 .H45 2002
953.8—dc21   2001053757

Saudi Arabia

Contents

Cover photo:
Bedouin sheikh
with camel

CHAPTER

Preparing for irrigation

Artifact from an
earlier civilization

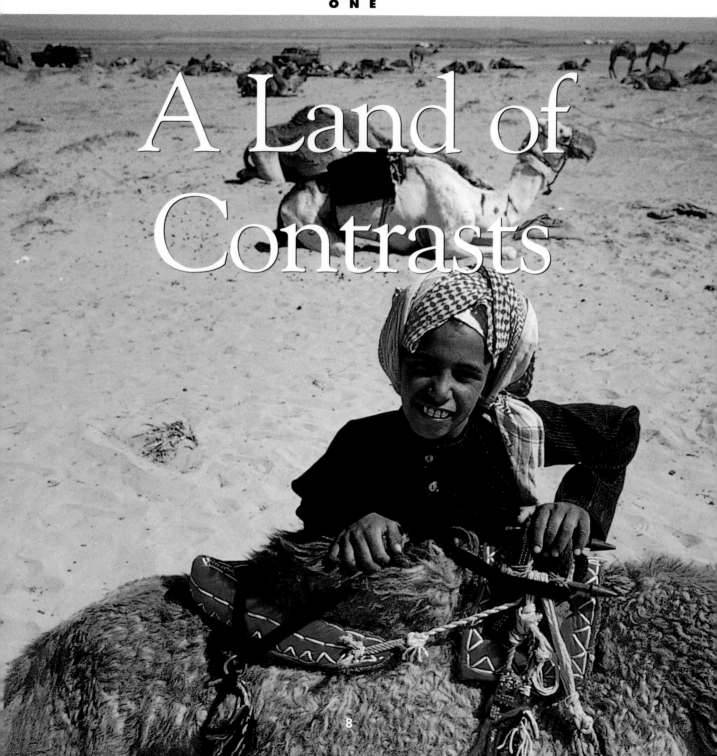

A Land of Contrasts

SAUDI ARABIA IS A LAND OF CONTRASTS, CONTRADICTIONS, and mystery. Side by side with its modern cities and industrial plants is a way of life that dates back several thousand years.

At nightfall, a boy from a nomadic Bedouin tribe helps his father feed and water their camels. By the light of a flickering fire, he will hear his grandfather tell tales from the days when his people were mighty warriors. In the morning, the boy will ride to school in his father's Mercedes pickup truck.

Opposite: **Camels remain a part of traditional Saudi life.**

Modernization and wealth thrive in Saudi Arabia.

A young woman in a high-rise shopping mall chats on her cellular phone. A black veil covers her head and face, and her black dress reaches to her toes. Around the corner, an old man who grew up in a thatched-roof hut surfs the Internet for weather forecasts.

In Saudi Arabia, you might see these scenes any day. But when oil was discovered in 1932, this desert kingdom was an underdeveloped land of scattered nomadic tribes. Its vast oil resources have made Saudi Arabia one of the wealthiest nations on Earth.

This Saudi man plots roadways for the growing country.

Skyscrapers rise over Jiddah.

Today, Saudi Arabia is the largest oil producer in the world. One-fourth of all the known oil reserves on the planet lie beneath its desert sands and coastal waters. Saudi oil fuels cars, trucks, ships, and aircraft around the globe.

Saudi Arabia's newfound wealth quickly seeped into every corner of Saudi life. Within a few short decades, glass-and-steel skyscrapers towered over sleepy oasis towns. Where camels had ambled across shifting sands, cars and trucks now speed over new highways. Modern hospitals, universities, factories, and telecommunications systems sprang up, as fine as any in the world.

While progress swept ahead with blinding speed, the nation remained firmly grounded in its traditional ways. Saudi Arabia is named for the al-Sa'ud (ahl sah-OOD) family, who first came to power in the Arabian

Peninsula in the 1700s. One promising son—Abd al-Aziz—unified the separate tribes into a kingdom in 1932. He succeeded because he and his warriors were united by the common bonds of their Islamic faith.

Today, as in the past, Saudi Arabia is saturated with religious culture and traditions. From the desert nomads to the king, Saudis share a strong religious identity. They cherish their homeland as the cradle of Islam—the birthplace of the Prophet Muhammad. His teachings introduced the faith of Islam in the seventh century A.D. Millions of Muslims—followers of the faith of Islam—arrive as pilgrims every year in Mecca and Medina—the two holiest cities in the Islamic world.

Thousands gather in Mecca for the *hajj*, or annual pilgrimage.

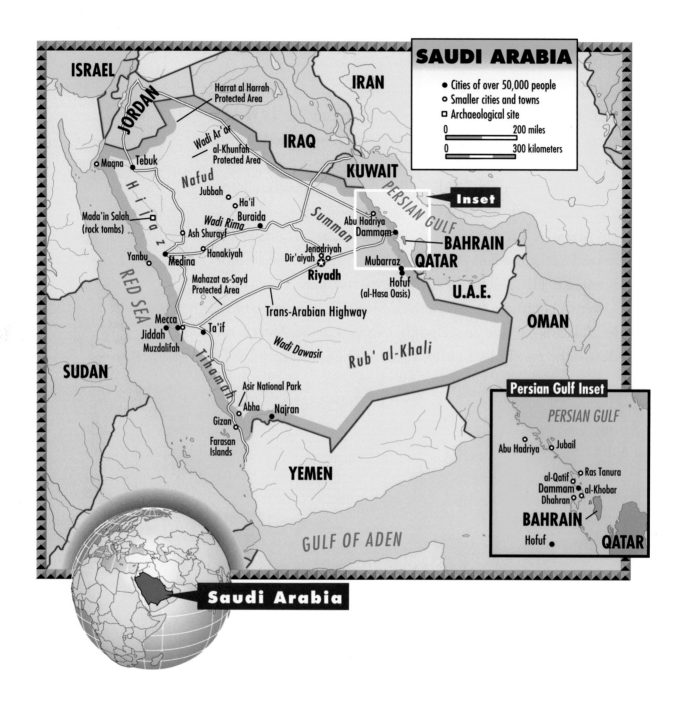

SAUDI ARABIA

- ● Cities of over 50,000 people
- ○ Smaller cities and towns
- □ Archaeological site

0 — 200 miles

0 — 300 kilometers

ISRAEL

JORDAN

Harrat al Harrah
Protected Area

IRAN

Wadi Ar'ar

al-Khunfah
Protected Area

IRAQ

KUWAIT

PERSIAN GULF

Inset

Maqna Tebuk

Nafud

Jubbah

Ha'il

Buraida

Mada'in Salah
(rock tombs)

Wadi Rima

Ash Shurayf

Hanakiyah

Summan

Abu Hadriya

Dammam

BAHRAIN

QATAR

Yanbu Medina

Jenadriyah
Dir'aiyah

Riyadh

Mubarraz

Hofuf
(al-Hasa Oasis)

U.A.E.

RED SEA

Mahazat as-Sayd
Protected Area

Trans-Arabian Highway

OMAN

Mecca

Jiddah
Muzdalifah

Ta'if

Wadi Dawasir

Rub' al-Khali

SUDAN

Tihamah

Asir National Park

Abha Najran

Gizan

Farasan
Islands

YEMEN

GULF OF ADEN

Persian Gulf Inset

PERSIAN GULF

Abu Hadriya Jubail

al-Qatif Ras Tanura

Dammam al-Khobar

Dhahran

BAHRAIN

Hofuf

QATAR

Saudi Arabia

**Geopolitical map of
Saudi Arabia**

This common religious bond has made the kingdom stable
and strong. Family ties are important, too. Since the founding

of the kingdom, all the kings of Saudi Arabia have been descendants of Abd al-Aziz. Under their rule, Saudi Arabia has become a leader in the Arab world and a respected moderator in the explosive Middle East. The Saudis also use their influence to keep oil prices stable throughout the world.

As prominent as it is on the world scene, however, Saudi Arabia remains one of the most private nations in the world. Non-Muslim tourists were not even allowed to visit the country until the year 2000. Only those with work permits and their families could enter the country. This reflects the government's desire to limit the influence of foreign cultures.

Saudi Arabia practices a very conservative form of Islam. Religious laws shape the entire government and legal system, with strict rules for dress as well as for public and private behavior. Clothing covers most of the body, alcohol and dancing are prohibited, and the holy cities are closed to those of other faiths.

With modernization came Western culture, ideas, and ways of life. All of a sudden, Saudis were exposed to drastically different types of social life, clothing, music, and personal values. Devout Saudis saw these influences as a threat to Islam—and to the nation as a whole.

Saudi Arabia today looks for ways to modernize the nation while holding onto its traditional values. The kingdom is committed to the latest technology, preserving peace in the region, and growing as a world power. At the same time, Saudis are determined to preserve their rich heritage and complex culture—now and always.

Spellings of Arabic Words

The Arabic language is written in Arabic script. For Western readers, it is transliterated, or rewritten by sound, into the Latin alphabet. Because there are several transliteration styles, an Arabic word might have several spellings.

This book follows the transliterations used by the Saudi Embassy and by *Europa World Yearbook* and *Encyclopaedia Britannica*, with a few exceptions. Names or terms that are familiar to English readers appear in their best-known form—for example, the names of cities such as Mecca and Medina.

Deserts, Oases, and Plains

SAUDI ARABIA HAS A GREAT VARIETY OF BEAUTIFUL LANDscapes. It has spectacular windswept sand dunes as well as luxurious coastal plains. Its rock-covered plateaus contrast with its lush oasis villages and their tall, graceful palms.

The kingdom lies in the Middle East, a region that stretches across western Asia into North Africa. It covers about three-fourths of the Arabian Peninsula, a great landmass that faces Africa across the Red Sea. Saudi Arabia is also one of the largest nations in the Middle East. This oil-rich nation is more than one-fifth the size of the United States and more than three times as big as Texas!

Saudi Arabia's neighbors to the north are Jordan, Iraq, and Kuwait. On the east, Saudi Arabia faces the Persian Gulf and the countries of Qatar and the United Arab Emirates (UAE). Bahrain, an island nation, lies just off the Saudi coast in the Persian Gulf. Oman curves around southeast Saudi Arabia, and Yemen makes up the rest of the southern border. In its far northwest corner, Saudi Arabia faces the narrow Gulf of Aqaba, looking across to Egypt's Sinai Peninsula.

Opposite: **Oases flourish here and there in this desert kingdom.**

Saudi Arabia covers most of the Arabian Peninsula.

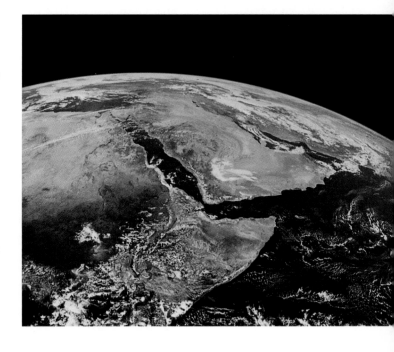

Deserts, Oases, and Plains **15**

The Empty Quarter's windswept landscape

Saudi Arabia is often called a desert kingdom, and desert sands cover most of the land. In the south is a vast desert called the Rub' al-Khali (Empty Quarter). Another desert, the Nafud, stretches across the north. In between is the central Najd region, a land of both deserts and mountains. The Najd slopes down to the low-lying eastern coast along the Gulf. On the west, along the Red Sea, are the coastal plains of the Hijaz. South of the Hijaz is the mountainous Asir region.

A wadi oasis in the midst of the Najd

Boundary Questions

Many parts of Saudi Arabia's borders are uncertain or in dispute today because of oil-drilling rights. The Saudis agreed on a boundary with the UAE in 1974, but its location has not yet been finalized. In a 1992 accord with Qatar, the Saudis agreed to set a boundary line, but that process is still under discussion. In the vast, desolate Rub' al-Khali, the border with Yemen was not defined until June 2000, but still no border crossings or guideposts mark where one country ends and the other begins. Also in 2000, Saudi Arabia and Kuwait settled a long-standing dispute over their maritime boundaries in the Gulf that involved offshore oil rights.

The Hijaz

The entire Arabian Peninsula slopes down from the highlands in the west and south toward sea level in the east. A mountain chain runs all the way down western Saudi Arabia, becoming wider and higher toward the south. These mountains are the steep edge of the Great Rift, a valley now filled by the Red Sea. Around Mecca, about midway down the coast, a break in the mountains separates the Hijaz region in the north and the Asir in the south.

The Hijaz has the holiest cities in the Islamic world— Mecca and Medina. It is in these cities that the Prophet Muhammad received his revelations and roused his people to follow the ways of Islam. Only Muslims may enter Mecca or Medina and their holy sites.

A few coastal plains lie in the Hijaz region between the mountains and the Red Sea. Over time, erosion has sheared off the mountainsides so that they come right up to the water today. *Wadis* (dry riverbeds) snake down from the highlands, filling with water during the rare rainfalls. Oasis towns have developed around underground springs and wells. Medina is the largest oasis town in the Hijaz.

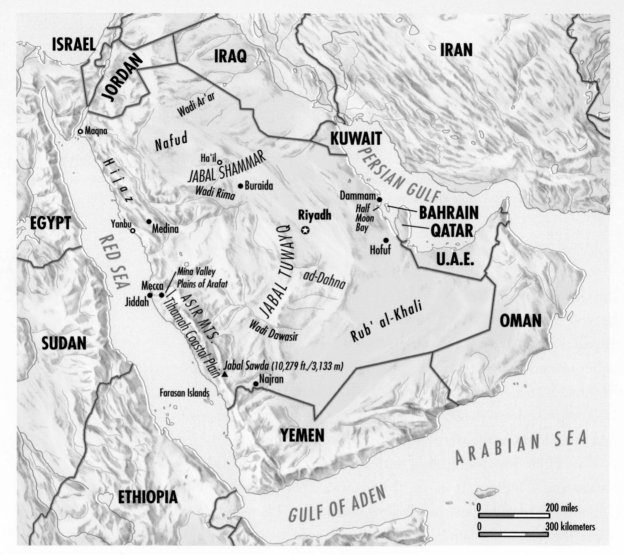

Geographical Features

Area: 830,000 square miles (2,149,690 sq km)

Highest Elevation: Jabal Sawda at 10,279 feet (3,133 m) above sea level

Lowest Elevation: Sea level along the Persian Gulf

Largest Desert: Rub' al-Khali (Empty Quarter), 250,000 square miles (647,500 sq km)

Greatest Annual Rainfall: 20 inches (51 cm) in the Asir region

Lowest Annual Rainfall: 0 inches in the Rub' al-Khali

Highest Average Temperature: 120°F (49°C) in July

Lowest Average Temperature: 32°F (0°C) in January

Longest Shared Border: With Yemen, 906 miles (1,458 km)

Greatest Distance North to South: 1,145 miles (1,843 km)

Greatest Distance East to West: 1,290 miles (2,076 km)

The coastal city of Jiddah is the country's second-largest city and its commercial and trade center. It is also Saudi Arabia's diplomatic capital—the home of its foreign ministry and embassies. Yanbu, farther north on the coast, is the seaport of entry for travelers from the west. In the mountains above Mecca stands Ta'if, the king's summer capital. Its cool weather and beautiful scenery make Ta'if a prized vacation spot.

The Asir

The mountains of the Asir are more rugged than those of the Hijaz. Saudi Arabia's highest point, Jabal Sawda, rises in Asir National Park near Abha. Abha is a popular resort thanks to its cool weather and mountain scenery. The Tihamah coastal plain lies along the Red Sea coast at the foot of the mountains'

Jagged and rough mountains of the Asir

steep western face. Some mountain slopes are terraced to make the best use of their fertile soil.

Najran, near the Yemeni border, is an oasis town where people have lived for about 4,000 years. Caravans carrying valuable frankincense used to stop here on their journey. The culture and architecture of Yemen permeate Najran.

Asir National Park

Covering 1.1 million acres (445,160 hectares), Asir National Park stretches from the Red Sea coast in the southwest up into the mountains and the desert to the east. Its scenic green mountains and valleys are a striking contrast to Saudi Arabia's deserts. Mountain goats, hamadryas baboons, and other wildlife abound here. The park's two main sections are the mountains in the northwest and the plains in the southeast. Abha is the main entry point. The highest mountain in the park—Jabal Sawda—is also the highest point in Saudi Arabia at 10,279 feet (3,133 meters).

The Najd

The Najd, Saudi Arabia's central plateau, consists mainly of high, gravel-covered plains, with stretches of sandy desert and clusters of mountains. Nomads graze their herds on scattered

Mountains overlooking vast stretches of desert and sparse vegetation in the Najd.

patches of vegetation. Farms cluster around the oasis villages where underground water sources nourish their crops. Many wadis meander through the Najd.

Oasis towns sprout up all along a high, arc-shaped ridge called the Jabal Tuwayq. (*Jabal* is an Arabic word meaning "mountain.") This area is the heart of the Najd and one of the most populated parts of Saudi Arabia. Its major city is Riyadh, the capital and largest city. Northwest of Riyadh, in the Jabal Shammar, live the Shammar tribes who once fought fiercely against the al-Sa'ud family for control of Arabia.

Beyond the Jabal Tuwayq is the ad-Dahna, a long, narrow band of desert often called the "river of sand." Although water is scarce, Bedouin herdsmen find pasture here in the winter and spring.

The Eastern Province

East of the ad-Dahna desert rises a barren, rocky plateau marked by steep rock formations and ancient river gorges. From there, the land slopes down to the Gulf coastal plain. This area is generally low and flat, with many *sabkhas* (salt flats). In the north are gravel-covered plains, while the sandy desert of the south merges into the Rub' al-Khali.

Al-Hasa oasis blooms within the dry expanse of the eastern plains. This is Saudi Arabia's largest oasis and one of its most fertile regions. Hofuf is the major city there.

Dammam, Dhahran, and al-Khobar are the major cities on the nation's east coast. Before oil was discovered, Dammam and al-Khobar were just tiny fishing villages, and Dhahran did not even exist. Now Dhahran is Saudi Arabia's petroleum capital and the home of Saudi Aramco, the national oil company. King Fahd University of Petroleum and Minerals is also in Dhahran. The town of al-Qatif is a center of the Shi'ite Muslim community. Jubail, one of the kingdom's two newly created industrial cities, was once a small fishing village, too.

The Nafud

North of the Najd is the great *Nafud*, which means "depleted" or "used up." In this dramatic landscape, chains of towering sand dunes stretch for miles, with broad valleys between them. The sand in the Nafud desert has a slightly reddish tint because it contains iron oxide. This tint is especially noticeable at sundown, when the sand seems to give off a reddish glow.

Few people live in the Nafud, but nomads can water their herds at its springs and wells. The town of Ha'il was once the home of the Rashid family, who fought the al-Sa'uds for control of the country. The town market and the ruins of the Rashid palace and mosque remain. In the far north, near the Iraqi border, the Nafud meets the Syrian Desert.

Red sands of the Nafud desert

The Empty Quarter

The huge Rub' al-Khali (Empty Quarter) stretches across the southern third of Saudi Arabia. This is the largest sandy desert in the world, covering about 250,000 square miles (647,500 square kilometers). Saudi Arabia's border with Yemen and Oman passes through the Rub' al-Khali, although no signs or checkpoints mark the border.

Parts of the Rub' al-Khali are flat, but its windswept sand dunes rise as high as 1,000 feet (3,048 m). In the west, the sand is fine and white. The elevation slopes down toward the east, where there are sand flats. Nothing grows in the Rub' al-Khali. Years may pass before even one drop of rain falls in this barren expanse. No one lives there, either, although Bedouins pass through on their migrations.

Water pumps continuously into this pool from underwater springs.

Oases, Wells, and Springs

Lush oases flourish in the desert where underground water breaks to the surface in springs and wells. Springs and artesian wells are scattered throughout the east and the Jabal Tuwayq. Large, deep pools in the al-Hasa oasis get a constant water supply from artesian springs. Thanks to this underground water supply, the people here are able to irrigate extensively. Wells are plentiful in the Asir and Hijaz regions, and many springs are found in the mountains.

In the Najd and in the deserts, however, wells are few and far between. People pump the water out or hoist it up in buckets or animal-skin bags. Also, because of salts and other minerals, the water from many of these wells may taste terrible or be completely undrinkable.

The Saudi government invests heavily in conserving and managing the country's water resources. By increasing irrigation, the government hopes to encourage Bedouins to settle down and farm. Another government project is desalination—removing the salt from saltwater to make it drinkable.

A farmer digs a ditch to irrigate his field.

Climate

Most of Saudi Arabia has a desert climate, with extremely high daytime temperatures that drop abruptly at night. In the central Najd region and the great deserts, summer temperatures average around 113° Farenheit (45° Celsius), and on a hot summer day temperatures may reach 130°F (54°C). December and January are the coolest winter months. Temperatures rarely drop below freezing in winter. January temperatures in the central Najd average 58°F (14°C), but high winds produce a biting windchill.

Thanks to the Red Sea and the Persian Gulf, the nation's two coasts enjoy a more moderate climate. In the summer, daytime temperatures there average around 90°F (32°C), while winter temperatures average about 60°F (16°C). Rain rarely falls in the interior, but both coasts receive regular rainfall. Humidity on the coasts is so high in the summer that a mist often sprinkles the coastal areas in the daytime, and a warm fog hangs in the air at night.

Vacationers enjoy the cool and pleasant climate of the mountainous Asir region in the southwest. However, people tend to avoid the Asir from October through March, when tropical rainstorms called monsoons blow in from the Indian Ocean. These monsoons drench the Asir with about 12 inches (30 centimeters) of rain every year—most of the region's annual 20 inches (51 cm).

Rainfall in the rest of the country is scattered and unpredictable. It often comes in a couple of downpours per year, flooding the wadis. The water disappears quickly into the sandy soil, where it is trapped between the surface and the underlying rock. There it nourishes the scant grasses essential to grazing animals.

Sandstorms and dust storms are natural hazards in Saudi Arabia. Hot, humid winds from the south bring a type of storm known as the *kauf* to the Gulf region. Another kind of storm, the northwesterly *shamal*, blows across the land in late spring and early summer. The shamal is especially severe in the eastern part of the country. For almost three months, its howling wind creates blinding sandstorms in the desert.

A sandstorm blows across the desert.

Looking at Saudi Arabia's Cities

Jiddah, a port city on the Red Sea, is the traditional entry point for pilgrims traveling to Mecca. The word Jiddah means "grandmother," because tradition says that Jiddah is the burial place of Eve. Saudi Arabia's second-largest city began as a trading center. By A.D. 646, Jiddah had also become an important seaport. Along the coast runs a 50-mile (80-km) corniche—a picturesque, park-lined roadway where people swim, fish, and picnic. Many of the city's older buildings are tall and narrow and built of Red Sea coral or coral limestone. Jiddah's old section contains the Souq al-Alawi, one of the finest markets in the nation, and Ma'mar Masjid mosque. The city's Municipality Museum is a 200-year-old traditional house built of coral.

Mecca, the nation's third-largest city, is the birthplace of Muhammad and the center of the Islamic world. The city, which lies east of Jiddah, was a caravan trade center that grew up around the ancient Ka'abah Shrine. Now the Ka'abah Shrine in the Sacred Mosque is the focal point for pilgrims making the annual *hajj* (pilgrimage). Other holy sites in the city are the House of Abdullah bin Abd al-Muttalib, where Muhammad was born; the Well of Zamzam; the tombs of Ishmael and Hagar; and a footprint of the prophet Abraham.

Ta'if, the nation's fourth-largest city, lies in the mountains east of Mecca. At an altitude of 6,000 feet (1,829 m) above sea level, this city is the king's summer home. Many other Saudis come to this pleasant resort town to relax and enjoy the profusion of trees and the scent of fragrant roses. The royal family of Kuwait stayed in Ta'if during Iraq's occupation of their country. Ta'if's National Wildlife Research Center breeds rare

animals such as the Arabian oryx, the Nubian ibex, and several gazelle species.

Medina, the fifth-largest city and the second-holiest city of Islam, is Muhammad's burial place. His tomb is in the green-domed Mosque of the Prophet. In the Qiblatayn Mosque, Muhammad received the revelation that prayer should be directed toward Mecca. Another religious site is the tomb of Muhammad's daughter Fatima. By 200 B.C., farmers had settled where the city is now located, and it was not until the A.D. 600s that the town was first called Medina. Today, farmers still grow fruits and vegetables near the town.

Dammam, near the Persian Gulf, is the administrative center of the Eastern Province. Before oil was discovered, Dammam was just a tiny fishing village. Now it's a major seaport, an oil and natural gas center, and the commercial hub of eastern Saudi Arabia. Modern suburbs stretch far from the city center toward al-Khobar and Dhahran. Together, the three cities make up one large municipal area. Dammam is famous for its gold market, and its Half Moon Beach is a popular tourist site.

Creatures in the Wild

ANCIENT ROCK DRAWINGS IN SAUDI ARABIA TELL US that a rich animal life thrived here in cooler, wetter times. From 8000 to 2000 B.C., the climate was much more favorable for wildlife and humans. People painted scenes of their environment on caves and rock walls, showing oryx, ibex, camels, ostriches, and many other creatures.

Some of the best rock drawings in the kingdom survive at Jubbah, in the Nafud Desert, and at Hanakiyah, east of Medina. Graffiti Rock, a site west of Riyadh, shows an ostrich with chicks, a long-horned cow, ibex, camels, hyenas, and a leopard.

Opposite: **An oryx from an ancient rock carving**

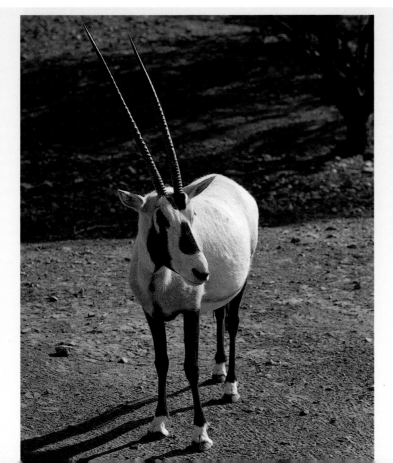

Saving the Oryx

The long-horned Arabian oryx is the largest antelope species in the country. These graceful animals once ran wild across Saudi Arabia. Hunting cut the herds down until only a few remained, finding refuge in the harsh Rub' al-Khali. The last known sighting of a wild oryx was in the late 1970s. Then the Saudi National Wildlife Research Center took some captured oryx and bred them. In 1990, the new herd was released into the wild in a protected area at Mahazat as-Sayd, near Ta'if.

Creatures in the Wild **29**

Great herds of gazelles once ranged across the Arabian plains, but hunting has almost wiped them out. The oryxes and the ibexes have also almost vanished, and the leopard is now rare, too. These wild animals quickly began to disappear as soon as hunters were able to chase their prey in vehicles. Today, the government protects many of these species.

Hamadryas baboons scamper across the rocky, forested mountains of the Asir region. These frisky primates have a highly developed social system, and couples mate for life. Mountain sheep, mountain goats, and wildcats roam through the highlands, too. Wolves, hyenas, and jackals survive on wild and domestic prey.

Hamadryas baboons play on rocks in the Asir Mountains.

Jerboas are tiny rodents that dwell in the desert.

Among the smaller mammals are foxes, rabbits, porcupines, honey badgers, mongooses, and hedgehogs. Hedgehogs escape the heat by sleeping in the daytime and coming out to eat at night. Sand rats and jerboas are small rodents that thrive in the desert. Sand cats live in some regions.

Cobras, horned vipers, carpet vipers, and puff adders are desert snakes whose bites can be deadly. Other species, such as the sand racer and rat snake, are totally harmless. Lizards range from the small desert skink to the large monitor lizard.

Saudi Arabia's coastal waters teem with fish such as tuna, mackerel, grouper, and porgies, and with shellfish such as

The cobra, a venomous snake, can be found in the deserts of Saudi Arabia.

A diver swims among the vibrantly colored fish of the Red Sea.

Creatures in the Wild **31**

shrimp. Exotic tropical species are found toward the southern end of the Red Sea. They include butterfly fish, leopard rays, Moorish idols, triggerfish, and clownfish. Many of these species have drifted north from the warm waters of the Indian Ocean. Fishermen who sail farther south, beyond the tip of the Arabian Peninsula, can catch sharks and sardines. Both dolphins and whales are spotted in the Arabian Gulf.

The Farasan Islands

The Farasan Islands, off the southwest coast of Saudi Arabia, harbor an amazing variety of wildlife. Their natural habitats include coral reefs, salt marshes, and mangrove swamps, as well as semidesert land. The nation's largest wild population of gazelles (pictured) roams here.

Dolphins, dugongs, and whales swim in the coastal waters, and turtles meander along the coast. Hundreds of seabirds nest on these islands, including ospreys, falcons, pelicans, and flamingos. Saudi Arabia protects the eighty-four-island group as the Farasan Islands Reserve.

An eagle takes flight in search of prey.

Saudi national preserves protect the ostrich.

Birds

Eagles, vultures, and owls are common predator birds in Saudi Arabia. The falcon, another predator, is caught and trained for hunting. Flamingos, pelicans, and egrets are found along the coasts. Small birds such as swallows, cuckoos, thrushes, hoopoes, ravens, and pigeons enjoy life in oasis towns.

Larks, sand grouse, and coursers live in the desert. Doves, quails, and bulbuls are common, too. Ostriches once lived in the Arabian desert, but the last known ostrich in Saudi Arabia was shot in the 1950s. Now the Saudi National Wildlife Research Center is breeding ostrich chicks and releasing them into the wild in protected areas.

Twice a year, birds of other lands pass through the nation on their migrations. In Jiddah, birdwatchers see huge flocks of Demoiselle cranes soaring past in the spring and fall. These birds cross the Red Sea on their flights between Africa and Central Asia.

Creatures in the Wild   **33**

Mahazat as-Sayd Protected Area

Mahazat as-Sayd Protected Area covers 850 square miles (2,200 sq km) near Ta'if. The entire area was fenced in 1990, making it one of the largest enclosed conservation areas in the world. The reserve is the new home for many endangered or extinct species revived by the Saudi National Wildlife Research Center. The Arabian oryx, which had disappeared in the 1970s, was released into the wild there in 1990. Wild ostriches began breeding there in 1997 for the first time since they became extinct in Saudi Arabia in the 1950s. Another endangered bird, the Houbara bustard, used to be a favorite target for hunters. It too has been reintroduced in the reserve, where it is breeding on its own.

Domestic Animals

Camels are the most valuable domestic animal in the Arabian Peninsula. In the past, a Bedouin counted his wealth by the size of his herd, and camels were his most essential trade goods. Thanks to their camels, the nomads were able to thrive for centuries.

Camels offer much more than transportation, though. Their milk nourishes travelers on long desert journeys. Camel hair is woven into fabric for clothing, blankets, and tents. And in a land where firewood is scarce, camel dung provides fuel for campfires. Camels also make good draft animals. They pull the ropes that haul water out of deep wells and drag plows through the fields. And let's not forget shade. On a desert trek, a Bedouin can take daytime naps in the shadow of his camel.

Sheep and goats together are known as *ghanam*. Sheep provide lamb and mutton, two favorite meats in Saudi Arabia. Goats' milk is made into cheese. Donkeys are useful for traveling and carrying loads, and chickens provide meat and eggs.

God's Gift

The camel's Bedouin name is *Ata Allah*, meaning "God's gift." The Arabian camel is a one-humped dromedary, unlike the two-humped Bactrian camel of Asia. Thousands of years ago, frankincense traders tamed camels and trained them to make the long trek from southern Arabia to markets throughout the Middle East.

Still prized as pack animals, camels usually carry loads of up to 330 pounds (150 kilograms). A camel's casual walking speed is about 3 miles (5 km) per hour, but a good racing camel can gallop as fast as 40 miles (65 km) an hour.

Camels can raise their body temperature so they do not start sweating until they're extremely hot. Also, they can live with little or no food or water for about a week. The foods they like most are dates, grass, and grains. The camel stores fats in its hump. When food is scarce, the animal draws energy from that fatty tissue.

A double row of long, curly eyelashes protects a camel's eyes from sand and dust. Broad, leathery foot pads keep its feet from sinking into the sand. The animal molts, or sheds its hair, in the spring. Camel hair is used to make clothes, rugs, tents—even artists' brushes.

Camels have a reputation for being bad-tempered, but they are really quite patient. The awful moaning and bawling sound they make is not a complaint—it's just their natural sound.

Arabian horses are known for their beauty and stamina. Although the breed originated in Arabia, only a few thousand remain there.

King of All Horses

King of all Horses, Drinker of the Wind, the Horse That Flies Without Wings—these are some of the ways poets have described Arabian horses. Arabians, the world's oldest purebred horse, are prized around the world for their beauty, intelligence, speed, endurance, and good temper. Nomadic tribes on the steppes of central Asia were the first to tame the wild breed. As the horses spread to the Middle East, Bedouin tribesmen bred them for their finest qualities. Breeding Arabians and racing them are still flourishing industries today.

Insects

The story of Moses tells of a plague of locusts that laid waste to crops in ancient Egypt. Locusts are a plague in Saudi Arabia too. These large, tough insects breed in the desert. Sometimes they rise up in swarms so thick that they seem to blot out the sun. Then they descend on farms and pastures, wiping out a year's crops in a matter of days. Swarms of locusts have been reported to fly as far as 1,500 miles (2,414 km) without stopping.

Bedouins, however, think of locusts as a tasty treat. They like the insects roasted, boiled, or simply dried in the sun.

Saudis have to deal with many of the insects familiar to other people around the world. Flies are common pests, even in the hottest desert regions. So are ants, beetles, ticks, and scorpions. In spite of the fragile flower-blooming season, bee-keepers raise bees for commercial honey production.

A Plain Tiger butterfly alights on a firebush plant

More than 150 species of butterflies also live in Saudi Arabia. Many are as exotic and colorful as their names suggest—Painted Lady, Plain Tiger, African Lime, Blue Pansy, and Yellow Patch, for example. Some of the most beautiful species live in the mountains and lowlands of the west and southwest. All butterflies in Saudi Arabia migrate over long distances. This enables them to get to flowers in different regions as soon as they bloom. But in Jiddah, with its parks and gardens full of flowering plants, some butterflies stay all year.

Desert, Mountain, and Oasis Plants

Most plant species in Saudi Arabia are well adapted to the lack of water. Some are able to store water, while others have ways to keep water from evaporating through their leaves. In the desert, grasses and small shrubs provide pastureland for sheep, goats, and camels. Some shrubs absorb salts from the soil. Their leaves give camels the salt they need to survive.

Many desert plants have developed ways to keep from being eaten, though. The leaves of the milkweed shrub and the bottle tree, for instance, contain chemicals that are poisonous to animals. Acacias defend themselves with their thorns. However, camels manage to nibble on their leaves anyway.

Clumps of junipers and other evergreen trees cover the mountainsides of the Asir region. Tamarisk trees thrive without much water, so they are often planted at the desert's edge to keep sand from building up in cultivated areas.

The Qur'an—Islam's holy scripture—calls the date palm a "blessed tree." Tall, graceful palms cluster in every oasis town. They are Saudi Arabia's most common tree, growing not only in oases but also throughout most of the country. Dates, the sweet fruit of the date palm, have been a favorite dessert and snack food since ancient times. People also use the date palm trunks for building their homes, the fronds for thatched roofs, and the leaf fibers for weaving.

Dates ripen on a date palm tree.

Wildflowers bloom in the desert after a good rain.

The Desert in Bloom

It's an amazing sight to see the desert come alive with flowering plants. It happens from November through April—the cooler, wetter season. After a good rainfall, flowering shrubs cover the rocky hillsides in the eastern lowlands, and the desert hills and wadis are lush with wildflowers.

Wild irises and many other flowers thrive on the silt that has settled in the wadis. Desert hyacinths, with their showy spikes of bright yellow flowers, are dazzling. Desert camomile, scarlet pimpernel, and heliotrope add to the mix of colors. Daisy-like anthemis and bright golden senecios are just some of the wildflowers whose roots help hold the soil so that rainwater can flow into fields and irrigation systems.

Along the edges of the harsh Rub' al-Khali, it's a surprise to see carpets of small pink and purple flowers. They're a desert-hardy type of forget-me-not. Ta'if, the summer resort town near Mecca, is famous for its profusion of roses. For years, the sweet smell of jasmine remains in the memory of many people who have lived in Saudi Arabia.

The Making of a Kingdom

PEOPLE HAVE LIVED ON THE ARABIAN PENINSULA FOR THOU-
sands of years. The earliest known people lived on the Gulf
coast north of present-day Dhahran around 5000 B.C. Their
artifacts are similar to those of the Sumerians of Mesopotamia
(now Iraq), the world's oldest-known civilization.

Until about 3000 B.C., much of Arabia enjoyed a moderate climate with lush vegetation. Deep wadis suggest that
great rivers once coursed across the land. But over time,
the climate changed and the deserts advanced.

Because of the harsh climate, people in the interior
lived as nomadic or seminomadic herders. Some grew
crops near the oases. Ancient historians tell us that
camels were common livestock in Arabia. By around
1000 B.C., Arabs had developed a method of sad-
dling camels so that they were able to transport
heavy loads over long distances. This opened
the doors to trade.

People who lived on the coasts were the
first Arabs to trade with people in faraway
lands. Those on the east coast made contact
with the civilizations of the Tigris-Euphrates
River Valleys in Mesopotamia. People on the
west coast had access to Egypt, Jordan, and Syria.
Arabia was in an ideal location to take part in the
caravan trade routes that passed through these lands.

Opposite: **Caravans once
traveled across trade routes
to distant lands.**

**Ancient artifacts remain
from early civilizations of
the Arabian Peninsula.**

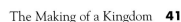

Ruins of the palace of the Queen of Sheba

Early Civilizations

Several great trade centers grew up in what is now southwestern Saudi Arabia and western Yemen. One was the kingdom of Saba, called "Sheba" in Jewish, Christian, and Islamic scriptures. Flourishing around 700 B.C., the Sabaeans were prosperous and built fabulous religious structures and irrigation systems. Their famous dam at Marib, in present-day Yemen, irrigated more than 4,000 acres (1,619 ha).

The Minaeans were a confederation of trading states. They operated trade centers as far north as Dedan, north of present-day Medina. About 100 A.D., the Minaeans' trade routes were overtaken by the Nabataeans. The Nabataeans had a magnificent stone city called Petra in present-day Jordan. Now, near Dedan, they built a new city called Mada'in Saleh. Carved entirely of stone, this ancient site is rich with remains of the Nabataean culture.

The Lakhmids, a Bedouin tribal kingdom, reigned along the east coast from the fourth through the sixth centuries A.D. An inscription on the tomb of a Lakhmid king declares him

Mada'in Saleh

The rock tombs of Mada'in Saleh are the most famous archaeological site in Saudi Arabia. Most of the tombs were carved out of solid rock between 100 B.C. and A.D. 100. Mada'in Saleh was then the most important Nabataean city after Petra in Jordan. The largest tomb, Qasr Farid, was cut from one large rock standing alone in the desert. A space called the meeting room was carved right into a hillside. The girls' palace, Qasr al-Bint, is a group of tombs. The hard rock has resisted water damage over the years, so the entire site is well preserved.

"king of all the Bedouins." Meanwhile, the Ghassanids controlled the northwest. They were foreign rulers with head-quarters in the Byzantine Empire (present-day Turkey).

Kindah, another Bedouin kingdom, was an alliance that stretched across central Arabia. The Kindites were in power as early as the third century A.D. They had trade relations and political ties all the way from present-day Yemen to the east coast. But by the early 500s, their kingdom was crumbling—partly because of wars, and partly because of the Quraysh.

The Quraysh confederation was formed around A.D. 500, when a tribal leader named Qusayy began to gather scattered Bedouin tribes together. He formed a trading alliance centered in Mecca on the west coast. One by one, the other trading kingdoms collapsed and the Quraysh took over their trade routes. Soon their far-reaching agreements opened Arabia to caravan trade with Yemen, Syria, Byzantium, Iraq, and Ethiopia.

Mecca was a major trade center as well as a holy place.

Mecca became not only a merchant center, but also a religious center. Its temple, the Ka'abah, was dedicated to many important gods and attracted pilgrims from all over the Arabian Peninsula. The Quraysh were honored as holy protectors of the temple. One especially powerful Quraysh family was the house of Abd Manaf. Descendants of Qusayy, they were responsible for raising the taxes needed to feed the annual influx of pilgrims.

The Rise of Islam

In Mecca, in about A.D. 570, a boy named Muhammad was born into the Hashemite clan of the house of Abd Manaf. Orphaned at an early age, Muhammad was cared for by his clan members. All of Mecca took notice when Muhammad began to preach. He taught that there were not many gods, but one—the one and only God known to Jews and Christians. His name in Arabic is *Allah*.

Muhammad gained some followers, but his new doctrine angered many of Mecca's Quraysh leaders. Without a multitude of gods, they would lose their religious place of honor— and their income from the pilgrim traffic. No longer welcome in Mecca, Muhammad was driven out in 622. He and a handful of followers found refuge among tribes in Medina, to the north. His flight from Mecca to Medina is known as the *hijra*, or Hegira. Muslims mark this date as the birth of Islam and Year 1 of the Islamic calendar.

After being driven from Mecca, Muhammad made his home in Medina.

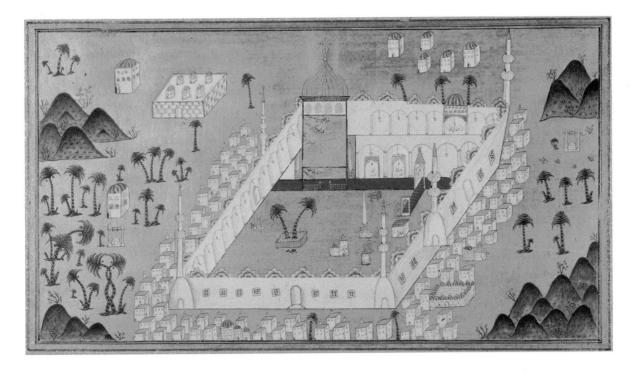

Muhammad gained many converts among the tribes in Medina. Soon a power struggle broke out between Mecca and Medina. The Quraysh attacked Medina but failed to take it. In 630, Muhammad and his supporters marched into Mecca and captured the city. Now both cities were sacred strongholds of the new religion. The Ka'abah, once a pagan shrine, became the holy shrine of Allah. Tribes once loyal to the Quraysh came to Mecca and pledged themselves to Islam, to Allah, and to Allah's Prophet, Muhammad.

Power Struggles

By the time Muhammad died in 632, practically the entire Arabian Peninsula was united under one rule. Arab tribes, with their new religion and a spirit of conquest, spread far beyond Arabia into Persia (now Iran), Iraq, Syria, and Egypt. But who would lead them after the Prophet died?

In this struggle for leadership, some argued that a relative of Muhammad's—a member of the Hashemite clan—should take the lead. But which relative? A son-in-law? An uncle? Others believed the position should go to an honored member of the Muslim community. Such differing points of view would divide Islam in the years to come.

Muhammad's successors were called caliphs. They were political, military, and religious leaders, although they were not considered prophets themselves. Neither of the first two caliphs was a Hashemite. By general agreement, Abu Bakr became the first caliph (632–634). He was a close friend and father-in-law of the Prophet and a respected elder in the community. Abu Bakr began Islam's expansion into Iraq and Syria and ordered Muhammad's revelations to be gathered together. His successor, Umar (634–644), was another father-in-law of Muhammad. He extended Muslim conquests into Egypt and Persia and set up systems for governing the Islamic empire.

Many Muslims thought the next caliph should be Ali, the husband of Muhammad's daughter Fatima. But the honor went instead to a man named Uthman (644–656). Uthman was descended from both the Hashemite and the Umayyad clans. (Umayya was a cousin of Muhammad's grandfather.) Uthman standardized the Qur'an, extended the conquests even further, and distributed wealth and power mainly to family members. Disputes about Uthman's leadership led to his murder—and a period of open conflict.

Ali at last became the fourth caliph (656–661). He ruled with justice and equality and fought off opponents' rebellions. But Uthman's relatives were out for revenge, and Ali fled Arabia for Iraq. With Ali's flight, the seat of power in the Islamic world left Arabia. It would never return.

Ruins of Old Town in Damascus

The Breakup of the Empire

The Umayyads, based in Syria, took control of the Islamic empire in 661. Umayyad caliphs ruled from their capital in Damascus and appointed governors to control sections of

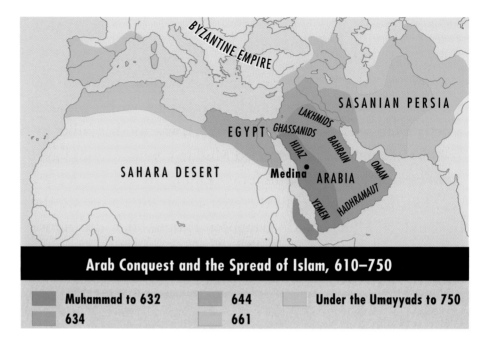

Arab Conquest and the Spread of Islam, 610–750

Muhammad to 632 | 644 | Under the Umayyads to 750
634 | 661 |

Arabia. In the Hijaz region along the west coast, the Umayyads invested heavily in the holy cities of Mecca and Medina. They rebuilt the holy sites and developed an extensive irrigation system.

Conflicts continued over Muhammad's proper heir. Two sects emerged—the Sunnis, who claimed authority through Muhammad's uncle Abbas, and the Shi'ites, who favored descendants of Ali. At last, in 750, the Umayyads fell to the Abbasids, a Sunni dynasty centered in Baghdad, Iraq. The seat of the Muslim empire then moved from Damascus to Baghdad, and the period of the Abbasid caliphate began.

By this time, Arab rule had spread west to North Africa and across the Mediterranean to present-day Spain. In the east, it extended into Persia, India, and central Asia to the borders of China. But the Abbasids could not control such a far-flung empire. Instead, each region was governed as an individual state. By 972, there were three rival caliphs—an Abbasid caliph in Baghdad, a Fatimid (Shi'ite) caliph in Egypt, and an Umayyad caliph in Spain.

As the political tides rose and fell, sections of Arabia fell under the rule of one caliph or another. In the Hijaz, the holy cities of Mecca and Medina continued to flourish as centers of religion and culture. Medina was a center for study of the Qur'an and of *Shari'ah* (Islamic law). Religious leaders in Mecca developed the rites to be observed during pilgrimages, following the Qur'an and the Prophet's *Sunnah* (traditions). The nearby port of Jiddah became the major port of entry for pilgrims.

Mecca became the capital of the Hijaz, and the sharifs, or tribal leaders, of Mecca made peace with each caliph who was in

Ottoman sultan Suleyman was the most significant ruler of his time.

power. When Mamluk princes took over Egypt in 1250, they claimed the Hijaz as a province. Still, they left the sharifs of Mecca with a lot of power.

Turkey's Ottoman Empire conquered Egypt in 1517. The sharifs of Mecca negotiated a deal with the powerful Ottoman sultans. The Ottomans would be honored as overlords of the Hijaz, while the Meccan sharifs would remain lords of the holy cities and Jiddah. The Ottoman sultan Suleyman poured massive resources into building projects in Mecca and Medina.

The Ottomans went on to take over most of the Arabian Peninsula, including Yemen and Oman. After taking Iraq, they controlled sea traffic on the Gulf, as well as on the Red Sea. For the Ottomans, the Hijaz was the most valuable part of Arabia because of its Red Sea ports and its pilgrimage traffic. They largely ignored the Najd—the great, arid plain of the interior. It was here, however, that great leaders would rise up to create an Arabian nation.

The Rise of the Wahhabis

With the Muslim empire split into so many divisions, Islam had moved far from its roots. This disturbed a religious scholar named Muhammad bin Abd al-Wahhab. In his view, Muslim leaders had become corrupt, and Muslims were slipping into idolatry and superstition. The only solution, he believed, was massive reform. Abd al-Wahhab began preaching a return to the original purity of Islam. But his teachings were too extreme for many, and he was driven out of his hometown of Uyaynah. He found refuge in the nearby village of Dir'aiyah.

Dir'aiyah, near present-day Riyadh, had never come under Ottoman rule. Its tribal chief, Muhammad al-Sa'ud, welcomed Abd al-Wahhab and embraced his strict teachings.

Arabian Peninsula, 19th Century

Ottoman Empire   British rule or influence
Wahhabite territory

Dir'aiyah

Dir'aiyah was the first capital city of the kingdom's royal al-Sa'ud family. It lies about 18 miles (29 km) north of present-day Riyadh and its ruins are the most popular archaeological site in the country. The walled fortress city of Dir'aiyah was founded in 1446 and destroyed by the Turks in 1818. Its palaces, city wall, and the Mosque of Muhammad bin Abd al-Wahhab have now been restored. The walls are made of cow dung, mud, and hay, just as they were originally. The roof beams are made of palm tree trunks covered with palm leaves.

Inspired with fervor for the Wahhabist doctrines, al-Sa'ud and his followers stormed through the Najd. It was both a religious and political conquest. With the Najd secured, they moved northward into Iraq and westward to the Hijaz. In 1806, the al-Sa'uds conquered Mecca but lost it again after a seven-year battle with Ottoman troops. The Ottomans took the Najd and destroyed Dir'aiyah in 1818.

A second wave of Sa'udi-Wahhabi conquest began when a chief named Turki captured Riyadh in 1824 and made it his capital. Turki and his son Faisal brought peace and prosperity for a while, but civil wars and more Ottoman invasions paved the way for a takeover. The Rashids, from the northern province of Jabal Shammar, took Riyadh in 1891. When Faisal's youngest son, Abd ar-Rahman, took refuge with other al-Sa'ud family members in the northeast province of Kuwait, it seemed that Sa'udi rule was over. No one could have imagined that

Abd ar-Rahman's 11-year-old son, Abd al-Aziz, would build the house of Sa'ud into a power known around the world.

The Making of the Kingdom

By the time he was 21, Abd al-Aziz had a plan—and he was ready to carry it out. He and a handful of men set out on a night march to take back Riyadh. In a dramatic raid at dawn on January 2, 1902, the city fell to Abd al-Aziz. He quickly regained control of the Najd. Now the family's original kingdom was back in the hands of the house of Sa'ud. But Abd al-Aziz had even bigger plans. This was only the beginning of a thirty-year campaign to unify all the people of the Arabian Peninsula.

Abd al-Aziz needed to instill a sense of unity and loyalty in his scattered Bedouin tribesmen. He himself fervently believed in Wahhabi principles. He knew that only religious fervor could inspire fierce loyalty in the Bedouins. So he established farming settlements in oasis towns, where tribesmen were schooled in Wahhabi principles.

By 1913, Abd al-Aziz drove the Ottomans out of the Gulf coast region, but they still held the Hijaz. When World War I broke out in 1914,

Red Type indicates principal tribes

IRAQ
TRANSJORDAN
RUWALA
UNAYZAH
SHAMMAR
BALT
HARB
MUTAYR
JUHAYNAH
PERSIA
Riyadh
QURAYSH
UTAYBAN
BANI HAJR
Mecca
SHAH RAN
QAHTAN
AL RASHID
OMAN
MUNJAHA
AL MURRAH
YAM
YEMEN
ABYSSINIA
Red Sea
ERITREA
Gulf of Aden
ARABIAN SEA

The Making of the Kingdom, 1902–1926

House of Sa'ud, 1902–1912
Acquired by 1913
Acquired by 1920
Acquired by 1922
Acquired by 1926

Sharif Hussein of Mecca allied himself with the British. His unlikely partner was British captain T. E. Lawrence, known as Lawrence of Arabia. Lawrence helped rouse the region's tribes in a revolt against the Ottomans. In 1916, when the Arabs destroyed the Hijaz railway near Yanbu, the Ottomans were cut off from the Hijaz once and for all.

Although the sharifs of Mecca belonged to the noble Hashemite family, they were no great friends of Abd al-Aziz. He wiped out Hussein's army in 1919, and by 1926 he had subdued the entire Hijaz. At last, after years of struggle, the Najd and the Hijaz were united under the al-Sa'uds.

On September 18, 1932, Abd al-Aziz declared this union as the Kingdom of Saudi Arabia, with himself as king. First he set to work consolidating his power and restoring law and order. He made every sheikh, or tribal chief, responsible for his tribe under the king's authority. Then he turned to modernizing the country as a growing power in the region.

The English soldier and author T. E. Lawrence in sheikh's outfit

King Abd al-Aziz

Abd al-Aziz (1880–1953), founder of the modern Kingdom of Saudi Arabia, reigned from 1932 to 1953. His full name is Abd al-Aziz bin Abd ar-Rahman bin Faisal al-Sa'ud. He is also known as Ibn Saud, and some called him the Lion of Najd. He gained control of the Najd (central Saudi Arabia) when he captured Riyadh in 1902. From there, he went on to conquer the Hijaz and Asir regions to unite the kingdom.

Through marriage, Abd al-Aziz strengthened his ties with various Saudi regions, and his many wives bore him dozens of children. After oil was discovered in Saudi Arabia in 1932, Abd al-Aziz developed a strong alliance with the United States.

Saudi oil refinery in 1956

Into the Modern World

The discovery of oil in Saudi Arabia in the 1930s changed the country forever. In 1933, King Abd al-Aziz's government granted Standard Oil of California the right to explore for oil. The first sizeable pocket of oil was found in 1938 in Dammam, near the Persian Gulf. Saudi Aramco (the Arabian American Oil Company) was granted exploration rights in 1944. After World War II ended in 1945, oil production began on a massive scale. With the help of the oil income, Abd al-Aziz built schools, hospitals, and roads throughout the kingdom.

When Abd al-Aziz died in 1953, his son Sa'ud became king. Under pressure from the royal family, Sa'ud stepped down in 1964. His poor financial management was creating serious economic problems. Sa'ud's half-brother Faisal then took the throne and made sweeping economic and social reforms. He instituted the first of Saudi Arabia's five-year development plans, launching massive industrial-development projects throughout the kingdom, and improving government services such as education and health.

Faisal was also committed to preserving Arab interests in the world. In the Six-Day War of 1967, he allied Saudi Arabia with Iraq and Jordan against Israel. After the Arab-Israeli war of 1973, Faisal rallied Arab oil producers to cut oil supplies to Israel and its supporters, including the United States. Oil prices rose worldwide, and with its new flow of income, Saudi Arabia began a dramatic transformation. This country, so recently a land of desert-dwelling nomads, became an urban, technologically advanced society.

King Faisal was assassinated by a mentally unstable nephew in 1975, and his half-brother Khalid took the throne. After Khalid died in 1982, Crown Prince Fahd became king. King Fahd had his hands full trying to maintain a delicate balance in the Middle East. His Eight-Point Peace Plan to resolve the Arab-Israeli conflict was accepted by the other Arab states, many of whom often disagreed on political issues.

King Fahd

Saudi relations with Iran remained tense, however, because Saudi Arabia supported Iraq in its war (1980–1988) against Iran.

The Gulf War

In 1990, Iraqi troops invaded Kuwait, Saudi Arabia's neighbor to the northeast. King Fahd asked the United States and other nations to liberate Kuwait. Thus began the conflict called the Gulf War. Using Saudi Arabia as their base of operation, U.S. troops poured in for what was named "Operation Desert Storm." Meanwhile, Saudi Arabia took in the Kuwaiti royal family and 400,000 Kuwaiti refugees. A combination of air and ground troops from the United States, Saudi Arabia, and a number of other countries drove the Iraqis out of Kuwait.

Supporting the Gulf War was expensive for Saudi Arabia, and not all Saudis welcomed the visiting troops. The more

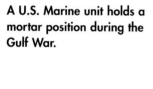

A U.S. Marine unit holds a mortar position during the Gulf War.

conservative Saudis saw the troops' non-Muslim culture as a corrupting influence on Saudi society. Others objected to warfare against a fellow Arab state. Islamic extremists were suspected of bombing several Saudi and U.S. military bases. In 1995, a car bomb in Riyadh killed seven people, including five Americans. Three dissident groups claimed to be responsible. Another bomb attack in 1996 killed nineteen U.S. soldiers near Dhahran.

Looking Toward the Future

King Fahd made sweeping changes in the government in 1992. He instituted a national constitution and the Consultative Council. He also changed the term of service for government ministers from life to four years. Of all his accomplishments, Fahd is perhaps most proud of his work in expanding and rebuilding the holy sites in Mecca and Medina. He declared himself Custodian of the Two Holy Mosques. King Fahd suffered a stroke in 1995. Since then, his half-brother Crown Prince Abdullah has gradually been handling more of the country's affairs.

Kings of Saudi Arabia

Abd al-Aziz (1880–1953), reigned 1932–1953
Sa'ud (1902–1969), reigned 1953–1964
Faisal (1906–1975), reigned 1964–1975
Khalid (1912–1982), reigned 1975–1982
Fahd (1923–), reigned 1982–

As it marches into the twenty-first century, Saudi Arabia continues its struggle to balance progress with tradition. On the practical side, Saudis are working to manage their growing population, their water shortage, and an economy that depends heavily on oil. On the cultural level, their challenge is to keep a balance between modernization and traditional values.

Governing Under the Law

SAUDI ARABIA IS A MONARCHY—A NATION GOVERNED BY a king. Its official name is the Kingdom of Saudi Arabia. The faith of Islam defines Saudi Arabia's national identity. Shari'ah, or Islamic law, is the basis for the nation's constitution, legal system, business affairs, and public policies.

Saudi Arabia's constitution uses the Qur'an and the Sunnah—traditional teachings of the Prophet Muhammad—as its foundation. Adopted in 1992, the constitution outlines the system of government, the succession of kings, and the importance of the family, as well as economic and financial matters. Human rights, like all other policies, follow the Shari'ah.

Opposite: **The royal palace in Riyadh**

The King and the Royal Family

The king is a member of the house of Sa'ud, Saudi Arabia's royal family. All members are descendants of the kingdom's founding father—Abd al-Aziz. By now, the royal family numbers in the thousands. Only direct male descendants of Abd al-Aziz can become king, and each king names his own successor. His choice must be approved by the Council of Ulema (Islamic scholars), the nation's highest religious authority.

Some countries have a king or queen who is subject to laws passed by a legislature or parliament. But the king of Saudi Arabia is an *absolute* monarch. That means he is the chief legislator (or lawmaker) as well as the chief executive who carries out the laws. His decisions, however, must follow Shari'ah and

King Fahd (center) speaks with his defense minister.

the constitution. The king is also the nation's supreme *imam*, or religious leader.

At some point in his reign, the king selects a crown prince as his successor. The crown prince must be closely involved in affairs of state to prepare for his own reign. Another top-level statesman is the prime minister. To assist in the prime minister's duties, the king also appoints a Council of Ministers. Its members are like the president's cabinet of advisers in the United States. The ministers reach decisions by a majority vote, although the king must approve their decisions.

King Fahd

King Fahd bin Abd al-Aziz al-Sa'ud (1923–), son of Abd al-Aziz, began his reign in 1982. He became king upon the death of his half-brother, King Khalid. Showing his commitment to Islam, he added the title "Custodian of the Two Holy Mosques" to his name. King Fahd encouraged Saudis to donate money and assistance to Muslims around the world. While preserving traditional values, King Fahd has also encouraged modernization. He has made great improvements in education, health care, and local industries.

The *majlis*—meaning "assembly" or "council"—began as a social meeting where Arabs gathered to discuss important issues. Over time, it has become a unique institution in Saudi Arabia. Now the king and other officials hold such forums regularly. Any citizen can come to a majlis and address his leaders with a complaint or a suggestion about policies.

It's a long-held Islamic belief that a correct decision is more likely to be reached by means of consultation. Seeking the opinions of those who have greater wisdom, more experience, and higher knowledge is a traditional decision-making style, from the tribal level up. This custom led King Fahd to establish a Consultative Council in 1992.

Today the Majlis as-Shura, or Consultative Council, is a permanent council of ninety members. The king appoints the members to four-year terms. Council members discuss important issues in the kingdom and give advice to the king. As with the traditional majlis, Saudi citizens can bring their concerns to the council for discussion.

NATIONAL GOVERNMENT OF SAUDI ARABIA

Executive and Legislative Powers

KING

CROWN PRINCE   PRIME MINISTER

COUNCIL OF MINISTERS   MAJLIS AS-SHURA (CONSULTATIVE COUNCIL)

Judicial System

SUPREME COUNCIL

COURT OF CASSATION

GENERAL COURTS

The Saudi Arabian Flag

Saudi Arabia's flag bears a white inscription in Arabic script that reads, "There is no god but God, and Muhammad is the messenger of God." This is the *shahada*, the basic Islamic testimony of faith. Beneath the inscription is a saber, or curved-blade sword, also in white. The background is green, the traditional color of Islam.

The shahada arose in the early years of Islam. Abd al-Aziz added the sword in 1902 when he became king of the Najd. The Najdi flag continued when the Kingdom of Saudi Arabia was established in 1932. Some versions of this flag showed two swords. The present flag was officially adopted in 1973.

The national emblem is a date palm tree above two crossed swords. The palm tree stands for Saudi Arabia's vitality and growth. The swords represent justice and strength rooted in faith.

National Anthem of Saudi Arabia

(Adopted in 1950; Words by Ibrahim Khafaji)

Hasten to glory and supremacy!
Glorify the Creator of the heavens
And raise the green, fluttering flag,
Carrying the emblem of light!
Repeat—God is greatest!
O my country,
My country, may you always live,
The glory of all Muslims!
Long live the king,
For the flag and the country!

Local Government

Saudi Arabia is divided into thirteen provinces. Each province has a governor, appointed by the king. All governors hold the rank of minister and report to the Minister of the Interior. A provincial council assists the governor and keeps an eye on the province's development. Provincial councils are made up of prominent local citizens. They meet in council four times a year, with the governor presiding. The 13 provinces are further divided into 103 governing units.

The cities of Mecca, Medina, and Jiddah have General Municipal Councils. Local citizens nominate their council members and the king approves them. These councils pass resolutions concerning a city's operations. Then the city's General Administration Committee figures out how those resolutions will be carried out.

Every Saudi village and tribe has a governing council, too. The sheikh presides over the council, which includes his legal advisers and two other influential people from the community. These councils have the power to make laws and enforce them.

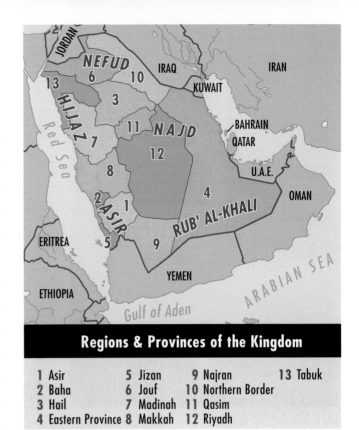

Regions & Provinces of the Kingdom

1 Asir	5 Jizan	9 Najran	13 Tabuk
2 Baha	6 Jouf	10 Northern Border	
3 Hail	7 Madinah	11 Qasim	
4 Eastern Province	8 Makkah	12 Riyadh	

Council members discuss policies and resolutions.

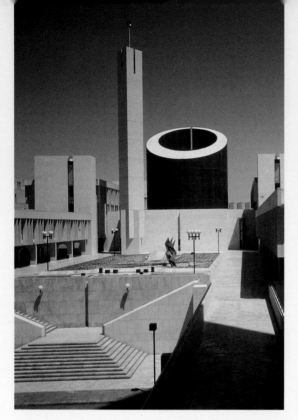

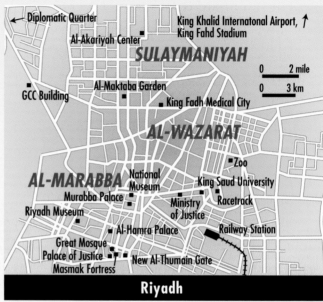

Riyadh

Riyadh: Did You Know This?

Riyadh is the royal capital and largest city of the Kingdom of Saudi Arabia. Its name means "the gardens" because it was once a small desert oasis. Today, Riyadh is a modern, high-tech city of skyscrapers, government buildings, and more than fifty public parks. Points of interest include King Faisal Museum, the Folklore Museum, and Qasr al-Murabba, the 1936 palace of the kingdom's founder, Abd al-Aziz. Some of the sites remaining from the old city are Masmak Fortress, the Great Mosque, and Qasr al-Hukm palace.

Location: In an oasis on the Najd, Saudi Arabia's central plateau

Population: 2,776,100

Capital: Of al-Sa'ud rulers 1824–1881 and 1902–1932; of the Kingdom of Saudi Arabia 1932–present

Altitude: 1,998 feet (609 m) above sea level

Average Daily Temperature: 61°F (16°C) in January; 104°F (40°C) in July

Average Annual Rainfall: 3.2 inches (8.1 cm)

The Shari'ah

The Shari'ah is the body of Islamic law. Its rules and guidelines cover people's conduct from the most private actions to public activities. Shari'ah was developed in the first four centuries of Islam by various judges and scholars. The main bases for Shari'ah are the Qur'an, or Islamic holy scripture; the Sunnah, a collection of the Prophet's traditional teachings; and *Ijma'*, a collection of Muslim scholars' opinions. Ijma' is used the way U.S. judges use precedents, or previous opinions, when they make their rulings.

Courts

Judges in Saudi courts use the Shari'ah in making their decisions. Trials by jury do not exist. Although there are no appeals courts, one may appeal a judge's decision to the king.

The Supreme Council of Justice is the nation's highest judicial body. Its eleven judges supervise the other courts, resolve legal questions, and review sentences given for capital crimes.

Cases that involve small penalties are tried in Summary Courts. More serious crimes are tried in General Courts, with one to three judges presiding. Only one General Court judge issues sentences, except in cases where the punishment is severe. Then all three judges have to agree on the decision. If a defendant contests the verdict of a General Court, the case goes to the Court of Cassation for review. This court consists of a chief justice and several associate judges. The Court of Cassation also reviews all cases in which the penalty is death or amputation. Such cases are also reviewed by the Supreme Council of Justice. Saudi Arabia also has specialized courts that handle matters such as labor disputes and commercial disputes.

Crime and Punishment

The Saudi legal system is known to be strict, and punishment is swift and severe. Under the Saudis' strict interpretation of Islamic law, crimes such as murder, rape, adultery, drug and alcohol trafficking, and armed robbery are punishable by death. The offenders are beheaded by sword in a city's public square. A thief is punished by cutting off a hand. Understandably, these harsh punishments keep the crime rate in Saudi Arabia very low.

Human-rights organizations around the world criticize Saudi Arabia for its executions, which number as many as 100 a year. Besides objecting to the method of execution as cruel, they charge that those who are accused do not always receive fair trials.

Law-breakers in Saudi Arabia are punished in a harsh manner.

The Religious Police

The *Mutawa'een* is the Saudi "religious police." Its formal name is the Committee for the Propagation of Virtue and Prevention of Vice. Members of the Mutawa'een are committed to preserving and enforcing Islamic law in its most conservative form.

The Mutawa'een operates at the grass-roots level—on the streets and in public gatherings. Seeing a woman dressed immodestly, a member might strike her ankles with a rod. Practicing religions other than Islam is forbidden in Saudi Arabia. Accordingly, the Mutawa'een have been known to break into non-Muslim prayer meetings and arrest worshipers.

A mutawa patrolling the Dir'aiyah ruins

While the Saudi government accepts the Mutawa'een's actions in principle, it does not always stand behind them. Under pressure from foreign governments and human rights organizations, Saudi officials sometimes prefer to deport offenders rather than punish them. The government has also instituted regulations to curb the Mutawa'een's activities.

Opposing Views

No political parties are allowed in Saudi Arabia. However, there are various opposition groups that challenge the Saudi government. Many of their leaders live outside the country for safety. Some opponents criticize members of the Saudi royal family for their corrupt and decadent lifestyles. Other adversaries are militant religious fundamentalists. They believe that Islamic law should be enforced drastically and absolutely. One such group is headed by Usama bin Ladin, who has operated from Afghanistan and Sudan.

Some critics believe Saudi Arabia is too friendly with Western countries such as the United States. They believe the government gives outsiders too much control over the kingdom's oil industry. Another complaint is that outsiders bring too much corruptive Western culture into Saudi Arabia. Finally, some Arabs find fault with Saudi Arabia for dealing with any country allied with Israel.

Neighbors in the World Community

Among its neighbors in the Middle East, Saudi Arabia is known as a moderate nation. Some of its fellow Islamic states, such as Iran, are more strict in religious and legal matters. Others, such as Egypt, are more liberal. Above all, Saudis want the region to be peaceful and stable. The major issue, for Saudis and other Arabs, is peace and mutual respect between Israel and the Palestinians.

Saudi Arabia is a generous "donor" country. It gives more foreign aid than any country in the world except the United States. Saudis give financial aid to more than seventy developing countries in Africa, Asia, and South America. These funds go toward building roads, dams, irrigation systems, hospitals, and schools. Other Saudi funds provide relief for victims of wars, famines, and natural disasters. For Saudis, this is part of the Muslim tradition of helping the less fortunate.

Shah Faisal Mosque, in Islamabad, Pakistan, was financed by Saudi Arabia.

C H A P T E R
SIX

Sources of Wealth

PETROLEUM IS THE BACKBONE OF SAUDI ARABIA'S ECONOMY. This desert kingdom sits atop the largest reserves of petroleum and natural gas in the world. About one-fourth of the world's known petroleum is in Saudi Arabia. Naturally, the country produces and exports more oil than any other country on Earth.

In a very short time, oil transformed Saudi Arabia from a land of desert nomads to a modern industrial state. The biggest change took place during the 1970s. World oil prices were high, creating a boom in Saudi Arabia's oil income. The kingdom invested billions of dollars in development. New airports, high-rise office buildings, and shopping malls sprang up around the country, and construction is still going on everywhere.

During the Gulf War, there was an international ban on importing Iraqi oil, so Saudi Arabia stepped up its production to fill the gap. This gave the country an even bigger share of the world market.

The oil industry accounts for about 40 percent of all that Saudi Arabia produces in a year. Oil also provides about 90 percent of the income that Saudi Arabia earns from its exports. The country's richest oil fields lie in the east, near the Persian Gulf, where oil was first discovered in 1932. Today, oil extraction

Opposite: **The oil industry has produced one of the richest nations in the world.**

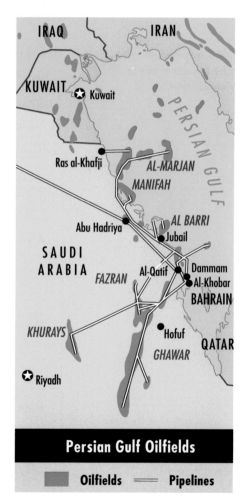

Persian Gulf Oilfields

■ Oilfields ══ Pipelines

centers around the Gulf-coast cities of Dhahran and Damman. The Ghawar oil field, almost 160 miles (257 km) long, is the largest in the world. Saudi Aramco, the national oil company, produces about 95 percent of the country's oil and operates wells, pipelines, and refineries throughout the kingdom.

What Saudi Arabia Grows, Makes, and Mines

Agriculture (1997)

Wheat	1,500,000 metric tons
Barley	800,000 metric tons
Dates	597,000 metric tons

Manufacturing (1994) *(value added in US$)*

Industrial chemicals	2,663,000,000
Refined petroleum	818,000,000
Iron and steel	516,000,000

Mining

Crude petroleum (1996)	2,933,000,000 barrels
Natural gas (1994)	37,701,000,000 cubic meters
Gypsum (1995)	337,573 metric tons

Money Facts

The Saudi riyal (SR) is Saudi Arabia's basic unit of currency. A riyal is divided into 100 halalahs. Coins come in denominations of 5, 10, 25, 50, and 100 halalahs. Banknotes are printed in the Arabic language on one side and English on the other. They come in values of 1, 5, 10, 50, 100, and 500 Saudi riyals. The Saudi riyal is very stable, and its value remains relatively constant. In mid-2002, about 3.75 SR was equal to U.S $1.

Saudi Arabia has great influence on world oil prices—including the price Americans pay for gasoline when they fill up their cars. When plenty of oil is on the market and prices are low, Saudi Arabia usually cuts back on production. When an oil shortage occurs and prices are high, it steps up production. Other oil-producing countries tend to follow Saudi

The Art of Money

Modern Saudi banknotes display a portrait of the king and scenes of important religious and cultural sites. They have elaborate decorative borders in traditional geometric and floral designs. Banknotes from the 1950s and 1960s have no portrait. Special commemorative banknotes issued in 1998 honor the 100-year anniversary, according to the Islamic calendar, of Abd al-Aziz uniting Saudi Arabia under the al-Sa'uds.

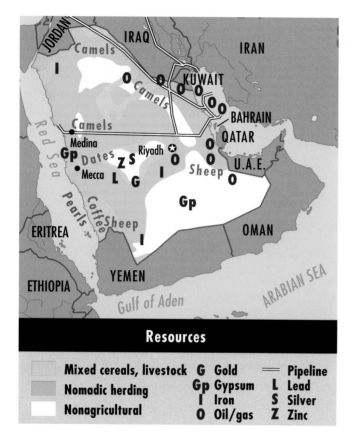

Resources

Mixed cereals, livestock	**G** Gold	═══ Pipeline
Nomadic herding	**Gp** Gypsum	**L** Lead
Nonagricultural	**I** Iron	**S** Silver
	O Oil/gas	**Z** Zinc

Arabia's lead. As the largest oil producer in the Organization of Petroleum Exporting Countries (OPEC), Saudi Arabia usually calls the shots. Iraq often makes its own decisions, however, regardless of OPEC's guidelines.

Other Industries

Saudi Arabia keeps some of its oil resources for use at home. This fits in with a wise economic policy—to diversify the economy by developing manufacturing and other industries. Jubail on the Gulf coast and Yanbu on the Red Sea were built up as industrial cities. They now refine petroleum and manufacture and export petrochemicals (chemicals made from petroleum). Petrochemicals are used to make a vast array of products, such as plastics, paint, cosmetics, drugs, explosives, and artificial fibers for clothing.

Factories in Saudi Arabia also make fertilizers, food products, textiles, clothing, cement, steel, and other construction materials. On a smaller scale, many private enterprises are engaged in baking, printing, and furniture-making.

Oil and natural gas are Saudi Arabia's most important mining treasures—but there are many more. King Solomon's

Opposite top: **Man at a weaving machine**

Opposite bottom: **Milk production in a milking shed**

Gold has been mined in Saudi Arabia for 3,000 years.

legendary gold mines are believed to have been at Mahd al-Dhahab, northeast of Jiddah. Gold is still being mined there today, 3,000 years later. Limestone, gypsum, marble, clay, and salt are among the nation's other valuable resources. Saudi Arabia also has deposits of phosphates, bauxite, zinc, copper, iron, lead, silver, tin, and other metals.

Saudi Arabia is beginning to privatize some of its industries, moving them from government-owned enterprises to private ownership. Telecommunications, Saudi Arabian Airlines, and port operations are among those industries.

The Labor Force

The unemployment level is high in Saudi Arabia, and it could get higher. About half the population is under age 18, and these young people will need jobs. The government is addressing this crisis with a policy called Saudization. Its goal is to replace 60 percent of the foreign workers in the country with Saudi nationals, but this is a tough challenge. By some estimates, more than 7 million foreign workers are in Saudi Arabia today. As a start, the country is stepping up technical training for Saudi nationals and asking private companies to hire more Saudis.

Why are so many foreign workers in Saudi Arabia? Partly because the country needs so many high-tech professionals. The oil boom grew so quickly that the education system was not prepared to deliver enough highly trained specialists into the

System of Weights and Measures

The nation's standard system of weights and measures is the metric system. For example, 1 kilometer equals 0.6 mile; 1 kilogram equals 0.45 pound.

South Asian workers on an oil rig near Riyadh

workforce. The only choice was to import professionals from other countries. As the twenty-first century began, only about 2 percent of Saudi workers were employed in the nation's massive oil industry.

Other foreign workers do domestic work and manual labor such as construction. With their newfound wealth, many Saudis are able to hire servants. Massive construction projects require tens of thousands of laborers, too. Saudis look to less-developed countries for workers to fill these needs.

Farming the Desert

Nomadic herding has been part of the traditional way of life in Arabia for centuries. Poor soil and lack of water made farming almost impossible anywhere outside the oases. Now, nomadic life is increasingly giving way to farming. Today, about one-eighth of Saudi workers are employed in agriculture.

The Gizan dam provides water for irrigation.

Almost all farming in Saudi Arabia relies on irrigation, and water is sometimes channeled for miles. Traditionally, most of the country's farming centered in the Asir region, the lush al-Hasa oasis in the east, and other scattered oases around the country. The government has dug and expanded wells and built almost 200 dams to provide

water for irrigation. More water is made available through desalination—removing the salt from seawater. These efforts have paid off. Cultivated areas doubled between 1980 and 2000. Now more than 12 million acres (4.9 million ha) are under cultivation. That's more than 2 percent of the country's total land area.

Irrigation of Najd wheat fields

Food self-sufficiency—producing enough for the country's needs—has been a major economic goal. Wheat is the biggest crop, and Saudis have been exporting their wheat surpluses since the 1980s. Saudis also produce enough dairy products, chickens, and eggs to meet their own needs. Barley, tomatoes, potatoes, watermelons, and cucumbers are other important crops, along with dates, figs, and grapes.

Herder with his goats

Camels, sheep, and goats are the main livestock animals. However, the Bedouins who herd them are finding it more difficult to keep up a nomadic lifestyle. Camels were once a sign of wealth and a form of money, but their prices have dropped over the years. A higher demand for sheep has helped the Bedouins, but they face stiff competition from sheep importers.

Many Bedouins take additional part-time jobs to make ends meet. They tend to stay near cities, where they can get jobs, medical care, and free education for their children. Since they no longer migrate to fresh grazing lands, they buy trucks to haul water and food to their animals.

Traffic is heavy in the city of Riyadh.

Transportation

Camels were once the easiest way to travel and the best way to transport heavy loads. Trucks and cars are quickly replacing camels today. In big cities, traffic accidents are frequent. Many involve teenage drivers, and some involve the occasional camel that wanders into traffic. Women are not allowed to drive in Saudi Arabia. Conservative

Muslim leaders believe this could lead to improper behavior, such as private meetings between men and women or violations of women's dress codes.

The Trans-Arabian Highway, stretching from Dammam in the east to Jiddah in the west, opened in 1967. Today, paved roads link all the major cities. Since 1986, travelers could take the King Fahd Causeway, joining Saudi Arabia and the island nation of Bahrain.

King Abd al-Aziz International Airport opened in Jiddah in 1981. Its Hajj terminal was specially designed to handle the annual arrival of pilgrims. In keeping with tradition, its modern design follows the graceful lines of a Bedouin tent. King Khalid International Airport in Riyadh opened in 1993, and King Fahd International Airport opened in Dammam in 1994.

Saudi Arabian Airlines, or Saudia, is the national airline. It flies to major cities in Saudi Arabia, as well as to New York City, Washington, D.C., and cities throughout Europe, the Middle East, Africa, and Asia.

Modern architecture of King Khalid International Airport

Tankers ship oil from Saudi Arabia to ports all over the world.

Saudi Arabia's long coastlines are perfect for shipping oil to world markets. Tankers can pass through the Persian Gulf or through the Red Sea to the Suez Canal. Ras Tanura, on the Gulf, is the major oil-shipping port. Jubail and Yanbu are heavy-duty industrial ports. Jiddah, on the Red Sea, is the major commercial port and the main port of entry for pilgrims headed for Mecca. The Gulf port of Dammam is the next largest commercial port. Gizan serves the southern Red Sea coast, while Dhiba serves the north.

Two women surf the Internet.

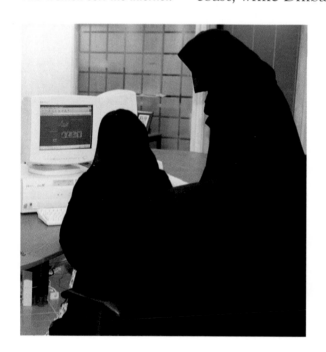

Communications

Internet cafes in Riyadh are packed. These popular access sites are an easy way for many of the country's 3 million Internet users to get online. Five times a day, however, Muslim users log off to say their traditional daily prayers.

Heavy security systems are in place to control Internet access in Saudi Arabia and to prevent access to sites that are considered offensive. However, many Internet subscribers gain access through the more liberal countries of Bahrain and the United Arab Emirates. It is estimated that about two-thirds of Saudi Arabia's Internet users are women. This may be because the nation's women have less freedom than its men do.

Saudi Arabia's communications systems are highly developed, but they are also carefully controlled. The government hopes to keep outside influences from weakening the country's moral standards. The Saudi Press Agency gives "direction" on how to treat sensitive news subjects.

Saudi Arabia's first television program was broadcast in 1965. Today, the nation has two channels. One offers all-Arabic programs, while the other includes English-language shows.

The national broadcasting service oversees all television and radio broadcasting. Saudi Arabia's wireless cable system allows the government to control the channels. Television satellite dishes are banned, although many households have them anyway. Thus, some people are able to receive CNN and other international networks by satellite. MBC-FM, owned by a member of the royal family, is the only radio station.

About a dozen daily newspapers are published in Saudi Arabia. They include three English-language papers—the *Arab News*, the *Saudi Gazette*, and the *Riyadh Daily*. Among those printed in Arabic, *Ar-Riyadh*, *Okaz*, and *Al-Jazirah* have the highest circulations. *Asharq al-Awsat* is a Saudi-owned international Arabic newspaper published in London, England. Several of these newspapers are also available on the Internet.

People with Common Bonds

THE PEOPLE OF SAUDI ARABIA HAVE GOOD REASON TO BE confident and self-assured. Their homeland is the cradle of Islam, and their oil resources are in demand around the world. Also, unlike many other nations, they are united by a common culture, religion, language, and ethnicity.

Saudi Arabia is often called a "closed" society. It's difficult to obtain Saudi citizenship, and as a rule, visitors may enter the country only to do business or make a pilgrimage. Not until 2000 did the country begin to allow very limited tourism. Once visitors are in the country, though, they find the Saudi people are open, friendly, generous, and hospitable.

Opposite: **The Saudi National Guard reinforces military and cultural Saudi institutions.**

The Population

According to United Nations estimates for 2000, about 22 million people live in Saudi Arabia. The overwhelming majority of Saudis are Arabs. They descended from nomadic tribes who have lived on the Arabian Peninsula for centuries.

The west-coast cities of Mecca, Medina, and Jiddah have the most

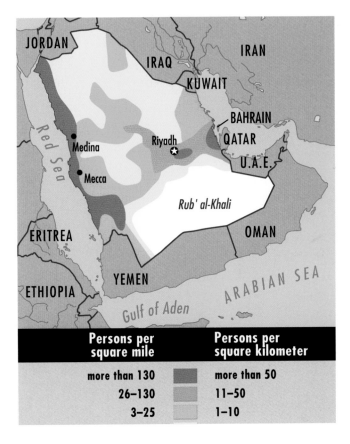

Persons per square mile	Persons per square kilometer
more than 130	more than 50
26–130	11–50
3–25	1–10

Some parts of Saudi Arabia have a diverse population.

Who Lives in Saudi Arabia?

Saudis	82.0%
Yemenis	9.6%
Other Arabs	3.4%
Others	5.0%

diverse populations. Over the centuries, Muslims from many countries came to this region as pilgrims and stayed on. Merchants—both natives and immigrants—built Jiddah into the country's biggest commercial city.

About one-fourth of the country's population are foreign nationals—citizens of other countries who work in Saudi Arabia. Some are professionals from developed countries, such as the United States, the United Kingdom, France, and Italy. They work in the oil industry or as teachers or medical workers.

However, the vast majority of foreigners in Saudi Arabia come from less-developed countries. They are recruited to take jobs that Saudis do not want, including construction and domestic work. Many come from other Islamic countries, such as Pakistan, Bangladesh, and Egypt. Others come from India, Sri Lanka, and the Philippines.

Where People Live

Before the 1950s, most Saudis lived in rural areas, far from the population centers. They lived as nomadic or seminomadic herders or as oasis farmers. Their tribal bonds were strong, and many villages were aligned with one tribe or another.

With the advent of the oil boom and industrial growth, people began moving to the cities for jobs. In many families, the men moved to faraway cities to work, while the women stayed behind to tend the herds or farms.

Now, about four-fifths of all Saudis live in urban areas. The most heavily populated areas are the central Najd, where Riyadh is located; the western Hijaz, with its cities of Mecca, Medina, and Jiddah; the Asir region; and the area along the Persian Gulf.

Population of largest cities (1995 Saudi census)

Riyadh	2,620,000
Jiddah	1,500,000
Mecca	770,000
Medina (1992)	608,300
Dammam	482,300
Ta'if	416,100

Modern apartments house rural migrants to the cities.

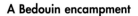

Those living in the city take advantage of modern conveniences.

City dwellers benefit most from the country's modernization. They enjoy modern housing, transportation, and other services, and they shop in supermarkets and shopping malls. Also, it's easy for them to take advantage of the nation's free medical care in modern hospitals and clinics and free education in modern schools.

For rural people, living conditions are quite different. Many live in small villages or farming communities that do not offer big-city services.

Saudi Arabia's nomadic and seminomadic herders are called Bedouins. Only a small number of Bedouins are able to carry on their traditional lifestyle today. They still follow the

A Bedouin encampment

The Arabic Naming System

An Arabic person's full name includes his or her father's name and often the grandfather's name, too. Just as in Western names, the given name comes first and the family name comes last. In between are the father's and grandfather's names. Each is preceded by *bin*, meaning "son of," or *bint*, meaning "daughter of." (Some transliteration systems use *ibn* instead of *bin*.) Some Saudis have no family name. Their given name is followed by only the "son of" or "daughter of" identifiers.

Example: Abd al-Aziz bin Abd ar-Rahman bin Faisal al-Sa'ud

Translation: Abd al-Aziz, son of Abd ar-Rahman, who was the son of Faisal, of the family al-Sa'ud

seasons, moving their tents and campsites from place to place for fresh pastures and water supplies. But the nomadic life puts good schools and medical services out of reach. Today, more and more Bedouins are camping on the outskirts of cities or giving up the nomadic life altogether, settling down to farm or moving to the cities.

The Arabic Language

Arabic, Saudi Arabia's national language, is spoken throughout the Arab world, including most of the Middle East and North Africa. Worldwide, more than 200 million people speak Arabic as their native language. English is taught in Saudi secondary schools, and educated Saudis use it in business and international dealings.

Arabic is the language of the Qur'an and the religious language of all Muslims. The Qur'an uses a refined form of the language called classical Arabic, or literary Arabic. The modern form of Arabic spoken today has undergone some changes over time to fit speakers' needs.

Arabic Numbers

wahid	one
ithnayn	two
thalatha	three
arba	four
khamsa	five
sitta	six
saba	seven
thamania	eight
tisa	nine
ashara	ten

Common Arabic Words and Phrases

Sabah al-Khair	Good morning
Masah al-Khair	Good evening
Assalaamu Alaikum	Greeting (Peace be unto you)
Wa-alaikum Assalaam	Response to greeting
Marhaba	Hello
Massalama	Good-bye
Kaif Halak? (to a man)	How are you?
Kaif Halik? (to a woman)	
Min Fadlak (to a man)	Please
Min Fadlik (to a woman)	
Shukran	Thank you
Ismahlee	Excuse me
Insha'Allah	God willing
Naam	Yes
La	No

Modern standard Arabic is used for formal purposes such as education, official business, and speeches. In everyday chatting, Saudis use one of the regional dialects. The Najdi dialect, the most common, is spoken in Riyadh and most of central Saudi Arabia. Hijazi is spoken along the Red Sea coast and in the nearby mountains. People in the Eastern Province speak the Gulf dialect.

The Writing System

The Arabic writing system is the second most widely used alphabet in the world, after the Latin, or Western, alphabet. Arabic script grew out of the ancient Nabataean alphabet. It is written from right to left.

The Arabic alphabet has twenty-eight letters, derived from seventeen basic letter forms. Dots are added above, below, or within a form to create the other letters. Three letters of the alphabet represent long vowel sounds, while the other twenty-five letters are consonants. Short vowel sounds are shown by a diagonal stroke above or below a letter or by an apostrophe-like mark above a letter. Letters can appear in different forms, depending on where they occur in a word. Some letters are shaped differently depending on whether they begin or end a word, appear within a word, or stand alone. Others keep their shape in any case.

Calligraphy allows the writer to make the script a work of art. Letters and words can be confined in a tight space or drawn out at great length. They can be large or small, with sharp angles or luxurious curves.

A sign in Arabic offers pilgrims rides to Mecca.

Education

Saudi Arabia has come a long way in a very short time in educating its people. In 1962, only about 2.5 percent of Saudis could read and write. By 1999, more than 90 percent of Saudi men and more than 70 percent of the women were literate.

All public education is free in Saudi Arabia, from elementary schools through universities. Grade levels are much like those in the United States. Elementary school includes grades 1 through 6, and students begin at age six. Intermediate school covers grades 7 through 9, and secondary school includes grades 10 through 12. Saudi children are not required by law to attend school, and about one-third of elementary-school-aged children do not attend. Many of them stay home, where their parents need them to help in the family business. Others simply live too far away from a school to be able to attend classes. Boys and girls have separate schools, and more boys than girls are enrolled. For many Saudis, a girl's education is not as important as that of a boy because her future is seen as centering on being a wife, mother, and homemaker.

Islamic studies are an important part of every child's education. School children also study the standard academic subjects as well as fine arts, and they take part in school sports programs.

When the oil boom hit, Saudi Arabia found itself with a large income but not many higher-

School children studying their lessons

The modern walkways of King Sa'ud University

level schools. In the 1970s, the country began a scholarship program that allowed college-age students to study abroad. Hundreds of thousands of young people attended universities in the United States, Great Britain, Germany, and other countries. Most returned to apply their learning in Saudi Arabia.

Meanwhile, the country invested in its own education system. It built thousands of new schools, including seven universities with state-of-the-art facilities. These include King Sa'ud University in Riyadh, the Islamic University in Medina, and King Abd al-Aziz University in Jiddah. Saudi women and men study for college degrees. Except in medical schools, women and men take classes separately.

The kingdom's specialized schools include the Higher Institute of Technology, King Abd al-Aziz Military Academy, and the College for the Arabic Language in Riyadh. The King Fahd University of Petroleum and Minerals is in Dhahran, and the Shari'ah College of Islamic Jurisprudence is in Mecca.

The Cradle
of Islam

I
T'S FIVE O'CLOCK IN THE MORNING, AND THE CRY OF THE
muezzin pierces the air. Men arise and leave their homes to go
to the nearest mosque for morning prayers. Four more times
throughout the day, they will answer the call to prayer. Even
at the height of their business days, merchants close their
shops and go to prayer, leaving their shoes at the door of the
mosque and kneeling on prayer rugs on the floor.

Daily prayers are just one sign of Saudi Arabia's religious
culture. Prayer times are dawn, midday, mid-afternoon, sunset,
and evening—not just for Saudis, but for Muslims everywhere.
When Muslims around the world say their daily prayers, they
kneel and bow in the direction of the holy city of Mecca.

Opposite: **Muslims at
daily prayer**

**Praying Muslims face the
holy city of Mecca.**

Religions of Saudi Arabia (1992)	
Sunni Muslim	93.3%
Shi'ite Muslim	3.3%
Christian	3.0%
Other	0.4%

No God but God

Saudi Arabia is known as the cradle of Islam. It is the home of Islam's holiest cities—Mecca and Medina—and the birthplace of Muhammad, Islam's founder and prophet. Islam is the major religion of the Arab world. Worldwide, about 1.3 billion people follow the religion of Islam. After Christianity, it has the second-largest number of followers in the world.

In Saudi Arabia, most of the population belong to the Sunni branch of Islam. They follow the strict Wahhabi version of Sunni Islam that originated in the 1700s. Other Saudis are Shi'ite Muslims. Most of the Shi'ites live in the al-Hasa and al-Qatif areas of the Eastern Province. Any non-Muslims living in Saudi Arabia are foreign residents. They are not allowed to hold public worship services.

The name *Islam* means "submission to God," and a Muslim is literally "one who submits." Islam is one of the world's great monotheistic religions (religions that worship only one god). For Muslims, God's name is Allah. The *shahada*, the basic Islamic testimony of faith is, "There is no god but God, and Muhammad is the messenger of God." Islam embraces many beliefs that are also found in Christianity and Judaism. It honors Abraham, Moses, Jesus, and other Biblical figures as messengers of Allah.

Muhammad, called the Prophet, founded Islam in the seventh century A.D. For Muslims, he was the last of a long line of prophets. Born in Mecca, Muhammad continued his teachings in Medina. Within ten years of his death in 632, the entire Arabian Peninsula had converted to Islam. Within

The Prophet

Muhammad, known as the Prophet, was born around A.D. 570 in the city of Mecca. He belonged to the Hashemite branch of the Quraysh tribe. Mecca at this time was a center for the caravan trade. It was also a pilgrimage center for those coming to honor the idols housed in the Ka'abah shrine.

Muhammad was orphaned as a child and lived for many years among the desert Bedouins. As a young man, he traveled with trade caravans. Then in 610, according to Islamic tradition, the angel Gabriel appeared to Muhammad and revealed to him the word of God. Now Muhammad began to preach *Islam*, meaning "submission to God," and its message of Allah as the one god. Muhammad continued to receive divine revelations until his death.

Muhammad's teachings were not welcome in Mecca. The idea of one god threatened the thriving trade that depended on pilgrims to the Ka'abah. Finding his life in danger, Muhammad fled with his followers to Medina in 622. This flight is known as the Hegira. It marks the beginning of the Islamic community—and the beginning of the Islamic calendar. He returned to Mecca at last in 629. By the time of his death in 632, nearly the entire Arabian Peninsula was united under Islam.

another hundred years, the Arabs' Islamic empire had spread west across North Africa and Spain, on the Atlantic Ocean. In the east, it spread to the borders of China.

The Five Pillars of Islam

Islam requires its believers to perform five basic religious duties, called the Five Pillars of Islam. They are: (1) belief in one god, whose name is Allah, and in Muhammad as His

Muhammad bin Abd al-Wahhab

Muhammad bin Abd al-Wahhab (1703–1792) was a religious scholar of Arabia's central Najd. With Muhammad bin Sa'ud, he set out to bring the region—and all of Arabia—back to the original form of Islam. The Muslim empire was split into several divisions in Abd al-Wahhab's time, and many Muslims had lapsed into idolatry and superstition. Abd al-Wahhab taught that all religious matters should flow from their original sources—the Qur'an and the Sunnah. Wahhabism is still the dominant form of Islam in Saudi Arabia today.

prophet, (2) prayer five times a day, while facing the holy city of Mecca, (3) giving aid to the needy, (4) fasting during the holy month of Ramadan, and (5) making a hajj (pilgrimage) to Mecca at least once in their lifetime.

The Holy Qur'an

The Qur'an or Koran is the holy scripture of Islam. Muslims believe it is the literal word of Allah, as revealed to the prophet Muhammad. The Qur'an has rules and guidelines for every aspect of life, including food, clothing, family relationships, education, manners, and business dealings.

In the Qur'an, the purity, beauty, and natural poetry of the Arabic language are at their finest. The book is divided into 114 *surahs* (chapters), revealed to Muhammad in either Mecca or Medina. Each chapter (except Surah 9) has a simple name and begins with the prayer, "In the name of God, the Merciful, the Compassionate."

A Qur'an with beautifully lettered Arabic script

Another body of writings—the *hadith*—is a massive collection of narrations about the life and traditions of the Prophet. Within the hadith is the Sunnah—the Prophet's teachings, sayings, and deeds. Together, the Qur'an and the Sunnah form the basis for Islamic law by which the country of Saudi Arabia is ruled.

The Brightness

By the noonday brightness,

By the night when it darkeneth,

Thy Lord hath not forsaken thee, neither hath he been displeased.

And surely the future shall be better for thee than the past,

And in the end shall thy Lord be bounteous to thee, and thou be satisfied.

—Translation of the Qur'an, Surah 93, Verses 1–5

The Mosque

A mosque is a Muslim house of worship. The basic form of a mosque reflects the home of Muhammad in Medina. It was a courtyard with small houses for Muhammad's wives along one

A mosque in Jiddah

side and a covered porch for shade along the other side. Mosques today have a *sahn* (courtyard), with a prayer area at one end and *riwaqus* (arched galleries) along the sides.

Every mosque has a high tower called a *minaret*. From here, the muezzin calls the faithful to prayer five times a day. Inside the mosque, the holiest spot is the *mihrab*—an arched niche that is elaborately decorated and framed by columns. The mihrab is carefully aligned in the direction of Mecca, following exact calculations. Here the *imam* stands as he leads the faithful in prayer.

For prayer services, rows of men face the imam—and the holy city of Mecca—kneeling barefoot on their prayer rugs and bowing low as they pray. In most mosques, women worship from the galleries along the rear sides of the mosque. Other mosques are partitioned down the middle, with men on one side and women on the other. Some mosques have an attached *kuttab* (elementary school), where children study the Qur'an.

Prayer rugs are used by Muslims when they kneel to pray.

The Holy Shrines

Saudi Arabia is home to two great shrines of Islam. The first is Mecca's Holy Mosque, whose massive courtyard encloses the

Ka'abah. This black, cube-shaped stone shrine is the holiest spot in the Islamic world. It stands on the 4,000-year-old site where God commanded Abraham and Ishmael to build a place of worship. All mosques around the world are aligned in the direction of the Ka'abah, like spokes of a wheel radiating out from the hub. Dressed in pure white robes, pilgrims on hajj circumambulate the Ka'abah, or walk in a circle around it, as they pray.

The other great shrine is the Mosque of the Prophet Muhammad in Medina. The Prophet himself founded this mosque in 622, and his tomb lies beneath the floor. The mosque has five minarets and a huge green dome. Only Muslims may enter the holy cities of Mecca and Medina.

Above left: **Worshippers surround the Ka'abah at the mosque in Mecca.**

Above right: **Mosque of the prophet Muhammad**

The following religious holidays are based on the Muslim lunar calendar and fall on different dates and in different months.

Ramadan (a month of fasting from dawn to dusk).

Eid al-Fitr (a three-day celebration at the end of Ramadan).

Eid al-Adha (a celebration of Abraham's sacrifice at the end of the hajj).

The Hajj

For Muslims around the world, the hajj—the pilgrimage to Mecca—is the peak of spiritual life. The hajj takes place from the ninth through the thirteenth days of Dhu al-Hijjah, the twelfth month of the Islamic year. It is the largest annual gathering of people on earth. More than 2 million pilgrims pour into Saudi Arabia every year to take part in the hajj. The feast of Eid al-Adha, celebrated at the end of the hajj, is the most important holiday in the Islamic world.

Pilgrims arrive by air, in buses, on camels, on foot, or through the Red Sea port of Jiddah. Only about half the pilgrims come from Arab countries. Most of the others come from Asia and Africa. Some villages raise money to enable one villager to make the hajj. On his return, he is considered blessed. *Umrah*, a "lesser pilgrimage" to Mecca, can be taken at any time of the year.

Ramadan

The holy month of Ramadan—the ninth month of the Islamic calendar—is a month of fasting. It commemorates the month in which the Qur'an was revealed to Muhammad.

From dawn to sunset, Muslims fast. They do not eat or indulge in other pleasures. After sunset, they break their fast with *iftar* (a special meal), say extra prayers, and enjoy a festive evening. Schools and businesses are open for shorter hours during Ramadan.

The end of the fast is a three-day celebration called *Eid al-Fitr*. This is the second-most important holiday in Islam, a time for feasting, getting together with family and friends, and giving gifts.

The Hajj Rituals

Certain rituals are standard parts of making the hajj. The day before the main rituals begin, pilgrims put on proper dress. They all dress in the same way so that no one's wealth or social status stands out. The *ihram* (hajj dress) consists of two seamless white cotton cloths for men and a white cotton gown and scarf for women. After the hajj, each pilgrim keeps the ihram for use as his or her burial shroud.

Next they go to campsites in Mina, a valley outside Mecca. They spend the night there in prayer and meditation, as Muhammad once did. The next morning, they walk to the Plain of Arafat. There, at the base of the Mount of Mercy, they perform the *wuquf* (the standing). On foot, and facing Mecca, they pray from noon to sundown, asking forgiveness for their sins. This is the spot where Muhammad preached his last sermon, and the pilgrims are joining his audience in spirit.

That night, on the way back to Mecca, pilgrims stop at Muzdalifah and collect pebbles (pictured). They will throw the pebbles at stone pillars in Mina as a symbol of their rejection of Satan.

Back in Mecca, pilgrims perform the *tawaf* by circling the Ka'abah counterclockwise seven times. They cannot kiss or touch the stone, but they bow deeply before it. The next rite is *sa'ay*—running (or walking) seven times between the hills of Safa and Marwa. This mirrors the actions of Hagar, Ishmael's mother, as she ran about in the desert seeking water. (Muslims regard Ishmael, son of Abraham and the handmaiden Hagar, as the ancestor of the Arab people.)

Before or after the sa'ay, pilgrims drink from the sacred well of Zamzam. The angel Gabriel is said to have opened this well in the desert for Ishmael and Hagar. Many Muslims fill bottles with the well water to take home.

During the hajj, each pilgrim sacrifices a sheep, cow, or camel. This honors the prophet Abraham's willingness to offer his son in sacrifice. (In the Jewish and Christian version of this story, Abraham offers his son Isaac. In Islamic tradition, that son is Ishmael.) Meat from the sacrificed animals is then distributed to the poor.

Once the animal is sacrificed, the hajj rites are complete. Pilgrims change into their everyday clothes and go back to Mina, where they pray or repeat the rituals. Meanwhile, Muslims around the world celebrate Eid al-Adha, the feast that honors Abraham's sacrifice and the culmination of the hajj. This feast is the most important of all Islamic holidays.

Arts, Culture, and Sports

DECORATIVE ART IN SAUDI ARABIA IS TYPICAL OF ART throughout the Islamic world. Islam generally does not permit picturing human or animal forms. Making these "graven images" is considered a form of idolatry. Instead, the artists use intricate geometric and floral designs. Their lines weave in and out, intertwining in exquisite flourishes and curlicues.

Elaborate calligraphy is rendered in pottery, sculpture, metalwork, glass, and textiles. Calligraphic inscriptions decorate buildings throughout the country, not only mosques, but also on office and government buildings and private homes.

An amazing array of handcrafted items are available at the *souqs* (traditional markets). Musical instruments, copper and brass items, jewelry, carpets, tents, and *mabakhir* (incense burners) are offered. Merchants set the price for gold jewelry by its weight. The amount of gold, not the labor or artistry it took to make it, determines the price of an object.

Opposite: **Geometric designs in stained glass**

Gold jewelry merchants in the gold souq of Riyadh

The Art of Calligraphy

Calligraphy—the artistic writing of Arabic script—is a decorative art all its own. In the early days of Islam, writing out verses of the Qur'an was a way to learn the holy scriptures. Out of this practice grew the art of calligraphy.

The traditional calligrapher wrote with a *qalam* (reed pen) or a *tomar* (brush) made of twenty-four hairs of a donkey. He made black ink from soot and colored inks from indigo, henna, nuts, and other natural substances.

Calligraphy remains a highly respected art form, and verses of the Qur'an are still its main themes. Inscriptions from the *hadith*, the Prophet's sayings and traditions, are common, too.

Skilled artisans used to be seen at their workbenches in every souq—carving, hammering, or engraving their wares. Now they must compete with imported goods. Their skills are in less demand and sadly, in some cases, they are dying out.

Scholars, Scientists, and Poets

Arabic became the language of learning during the Middle Ages. Brilliant Muslim scholars set up centers of learning in Baghdad, Iraq; Damascus, Syria; Alexandria, Egypt; and Cordoba, Spain.

Here they translated ancient Persian, Indian, and Greek writings into Arabic. As Western scholars began to discover these translations, they in turn translated them into Latin. In this way, the West gained access to the works of many great thinkers of the ancient world, such as the Greek philosopher Aristotle.

Arabic scientists also explored the fields of astronomy, mathematics, and physics. Arabic astronomers discovered and named new stars, many of which still have their Arabic names today. The ninth-century mathematician al-Khwarazmi introduced Arabic numerals to Europeans. Those numerals developed into the numbers now used throughout most of the world. The word *algebra* comes from the title of one of his mathematics books, and the word *algorithm* comes from his name.

Poetry is an ancient tradition among the Arabs. Epic poems of love, war, and honor have been passed down for generations. A storyteller wove enchanting tales for the audience that gathered around him. Famous epic poems still survive in beautiful illuminated manuscripts—books in ornamental handwriting decorated with rich colors and gold-leaf designs.

The Man Who Would Be a Prophet

Al-Mutanabbi (Abu at-Tayyib Ahmad bin Husayn al-Mutanabbi) [915–965] is widely considered the greatest of the classical Arab poets. Born in Iraq and educated in Damascus, he lived for a time with a Bedouin tribe. He was imprisoned as a young man for saying he was a prophet and writing verses that imitated the Qur'an. Thus he was given his name, which means "he who claims to be a prophet." While in jail, al-Mutanabbi began to write poetry in earnest. He developed a style that was very flowery while keeping to strict rules of meter and rhyme. Al-Mutanabbi later served as the court poet for various princes in Syria, Egypt, and Persia. He was an expert at satires and panegyrics (poems of exaggerated praise). At the same time, his skillful and ornate style honored poetic tradition.

The Arabian Nights

What do Aladdin, Ali Baba, and Sindbad the Sailor have in common? They are all characters in a massive story collection called *The Arabian Nights* or *The Thousand and One Nights*. In these stories, a beautiful lady named Scheherazade must entertain the sultan with stories night after night to keep from being executed.

Fairy tales, fables, legends, romances, and thrilling adventure tales—all these are found in *The Arabian Nights*. The stories have been told and retold for centuries and translated into countless languages. People young and old have enjoyed them in written form as well as in operas, plays, television shows, and movies.

No one can figure out exactly how or where these stories originated. Although many are set in Baghdad, Iraq, others seem to come from Egypt, Arabia, India, Persia, Israel, and Greece. It is believed that they were first written down in Egypt in the 1300s.

Music and Dance

Saudi folk music varies from one region to another. The national dance is the *ardha*, a men's sword dance that began in the central Najd region. The swordsmen dance shoulder-to-shoulder as a poet sings traditional verses to the rhythm of drums.

The *al-sihba* folk music of the Hijaz uses exotic songs and poems of Spain from the time of Arabic rule. In Mecca, Medina, and Jiddah, people perform a traditional dance to the strains of the *al-mizmar*, similar to the Western oboe.

The ardha being performed by swordsmen

Another classical Arabian instrument is the *oud*. It was the ancestor of the European lute. In fact, the word *lute* comes from the Arabic *al-oud*. It has a pear-shaped wooden body and four to six pairs of strings plucked with a pick.

The *tablah* is a small earthenware or metal drum with goat or fish skin stretched over it. A *qanum* is a trapezoid-shaped board with eighty-one strings stretched across it. It's placed on a table or on the lap. The *nay* is a reed pipe, and the *mijwiz* is a double-reed clarinet.

Modern Saudi music has an unmistakable Arabic sound. Today's songwriters draw on the sounds and rhythms of their ancient musical heritage. Although the words are new, the sharp intonations, exotic melody lines, and driving rhythms are traditional.

Saudi musicians playing traditional instruments

The Jenadriyah Heritage and Cultural Festival

Traditional camel races open the Jenadriyah Heritage and Cultural Festival. This two-week festival outside Riyadh celebrates Saudi Arabia's traditions and culture. Folklore troupes showcase traditional folk music and national dances such the ardha. Saudi poets compete in the festival, too. Artisans such as potters, woodworkers, and weavers demonstrate their crafts on porches with typical palm-frond roofs. More than a million Saudis attend the festival each year, and Jenadriyah now has a permanent, year-round heritage village.

Homes and Building Styles

Old homes in a Jiddah alley

Traditionally, buildings in Saudi Arabia were made with the most easily available materials in a region. Adobe, or sun-dried mud brick, is often seen in central and eastern Saudi Arabia. An adobe house provides good insulation from the heat. In the west, buildings are usually made of stone and red brick. The pinkish buildings in Jiddah, along the Red Sea, are made of coral from the region's offshore reefs.

Housing styles in different regions show interesting variations. In the Abha region, for instance, women paint brightly colored geometric and floral patterns along the rooftops and around the doors and windows. They paint once a year, usually to get ready for the celebrations after Ramadan. Today the women use synthetic paints, but in the past they used a variety of plants and minerals to make paint. Red paint came from clay or pomegranate juice. Boiling indigo plants produced a blue color, while green came from alfalfa or clove plants and black came from vegetable tar.

Saudi Arabia's mosques are the nation's most beautiful and decorative structures. They feature mosaics, colored tiles, decoratively cut stone or plaster, walls of open latticework, and doors and windows with arches at the top. Many of these same features are also in public buildings and upper-class homes.

In the 1960s, city architecture styles began to change. New office buildings and houses featured stark, straight lines. At the same time, they kept many traditional design features. The airport terminals at Riyadh and Jiddah are striking examples of Saudi Arabia's modern architecture.

King Abd al-Aziz Historical Center

The King Abd al-Aziz Historical Center opened in Riyadh in December 1998. It celebrates the 100-year anniversary, by the Islamic calendar, of the king's capture of Riyadh in 1902. This date was the first step in the founding of the Kingdom of Saudi Arabia.

A new national museum serves as the centerpiece of the sprawling complex. Its galleries showcase the natural and human history of the Arabian Peninsula, especially the rise of Islam and the house of al-Sa'ud. The center's public park is arranged as five gardens with rich, green landscaping, shady courtyards, palm groves, and play areas.

Another building, the Daarat al-Malik Abd al-Aziz, houses artifacts and personal belongings of the king. Other areas in the building include a women's research center and a magazine publishing house. Surrounding mud houses dating from this time display cultural exhibitions.

The Masmak Fortress, a mud fort built around 1865, features a reconstructed *diwan*, or sitting room. The King Abd al-Aziz Library and Auditorium complete the memorial complex.

Sports: An Ancient Tradition

People of the Arabian Peninsula have enjoyed sports for thousands of years. Ancient writings tell of great horse races, camel races, falconry, and hunting events. Many of these traditional sports are still popular today.

Arabian horses are prized all over the world for their beauty, intelligence, and speed. In Saudi Arabia, they race before huge crowds. Betting, however, is not allowed because Islam forbids gambling. Bedouins once raced thunderous herds of camels across the desert. Today, camel races are still well attended. Every Monday throughout the winter, camel races are held in the King Fahd Stadium in Riyadh. As many as 30,000 spectators gather there for the annual King's Camel Race, one of the most famous in the world.

Camels run for the finish line in the King's Camel Race.

A falconer prepares his bird for flight.

Hunting wild game grew from a survival skill to a sport. Hunting sports include archery and falconry. Falconry, which has a long tradition in Arabia, central Asia, and India, is a form of hunting that uses a falcon to snare the prey. Falcons are elegant, powerful birds that look a lot like hawks and eagles. The falconer, wearing a thick leather glove, trains the bird to follow commands for capturing prey and returning to his hand.

Besides traditional sports, Saudis enjoy soccer, volleyball, and basketball. The most popular sport is soccer. Almost every town has its own soccer league and field. Saudi Arabia's

The Noble Dog

To track and chase wild animals, Arabian hunters relied on the sleek saluki hound. The saluki, also called the gazelle hound, is named for the ancient Arabian city of Saluq. It's believed to be the first dog species trained as a domestic animal. Ancient carvings reveal that salukis may have been around as early as 7000 B.C. Both the Prophet Muhammad and Cleopatra, Queen of Egypt, are said to have owned salukis. Arabs called the saluki the "noble one" and used the dog to hunt gazelles. Salukis run easily over rough terrain to catch gazelles, hares, and other fast-running animals.

Saudi Arabia's national soccer team during the Asian Cup 2000.

national soccer team took part in the 1994 and 1998 World Cup Soccer Championships and qualified for the 1996 Olympic Games. In Saudi Arabia, only men and boys play soccer or attend the games as spectators.

Young people can take part in sports programs in schools. In addition, many have sports facilities and playgrounds in their neighborhoods. Even in smaller towns, young people can join sports clubs that offer soccer, volleyball, basketball, swimming, wrestling, and many other sports. Saudi athletes can join leagues and compete in local, regional, and national events. The best athletes go on to compete in more than forty international sports events.

Fifteen cities around the country have gigantic sports complexes called Sports Cities. They include huge stadiums that seat thousands, as well as Olympic-size swimming pools, tennis courts, playgrounds, and sports medicine clinics. The King Fahd Stadium in Riyadh is the best-known Sports City.

The well-known King Fahd Sports Complex

A World-Class Hurdle

Saudis celebrated their first-ever Olympic victory in the 2000 Summer Olympic Games in Sydney, Australia. Track-and-field contender Hadi Souan Somayli took the silver medal in the 400-meter hurdle. He was the first Saudi athlete ever to make the finals in an Olympic event. Somayli's impressive 47.53-second time set a new Asian record. "Of course, I felt initially disappointed at not getting the gold," Somayli said, "but this is quite amazing!"

With long coastlines on the east and west, Saudis enjoy water sports. Scuba divers and snorkelers explore the spectacular coral reefs off both coasts. Sailing, windsurfing, and waterskiing are popular, and the Red Sea is prized for its deep-sea fishing. On the Gulf coast, Ras Tanura and Half Moon Bay are favorite resort areas.

In this desert kingdom, the desert has its attractions, too. Many people take to the desert for outings to archaeological sites, or even for picnics. They enjoy getting back in touch with the traditions and simple joys of their ancestors.

Living from Day to Day

DAILY LIFE IN SAUDI ARABIA IS A MIX OF ANCIENT AND modern cultures. For example, women veiled from head to toe chat on their cell phones. Or a shiny new Mercedes truck zooms by, carrying a herd of camels.

In the cities, many residents live in high-rise apartment buildings. Wealthier people live in single-family homes. Some of these homes are surrounded by high walls that enclose lush gardens with fountains, babbling waterfalls, and rippling streams. Floors are covered with hand-woven carpets and cushions, and colorful hangings adorn the walls.

Cars, buses, and taxis fill the streets in downtown areas, and new construction is going on everywhere. The souqs are alive with the crunch and bustle of shoppers and the sounds of hard bargaining. Saudis can also shop in glistening, multilevel shopping complexes with hundreds of shops. Some of them have play areas where children can have fun while their mothers shop.

Opposite: **Ancient and modern cultures exist side by side in everyday life.**

The number of Western-style shopping malls is growing in Saudi Arabia.

A Different Way of Life

At the other extreme are Saudi Arabia's Bedouin people. Their homes are tents with wooden frames, draped with strips

Bedouin men sit inside their tent.

of cloth woven from goat hair. The tent protects the family from wind, rain, heat, and cold. Curtains divide the public area of the tent from the family's living section. Scattered about are beautiful carpets the women have woven by hand.

The Bedouin are organized into tribes, which are divided into many clans and sub-clans. A sheikh is the leader of a tribe. He consults with other tribal members for advice in making decisions. Tribal consultation in an open majlis is a Saudi tradition practiced on the highest government levels.

Traditionally, the Bedouin migrate across the deserts with their animals. When they reach good pastureland with a nearby water supply, they pitch camp and stay until it's time to move to fresh pastures. These migrations usually follow the change of seasons. After the winter rains, a carpet of lush, green grass covers parts of the desert. Herds can graze there until the summer heat dries it up. Then they move to oases, well sites, or plateaus where plants still survive.

Modern times have brought many changes in the nomads' lifestyle. Camels have given way to pickup trucks and cars. Now the Bedouin transport water and food to their animals instead of

National Holidays in Saudi Arabia

Eid al-Fitr   End of Ramadan
Eid al-Adha End of the Hajj

herding the livestock to greener pastures. When they move, trucks are more likely than camels to be their "pack animals." The animals may even make the trip in a pickup truck. To be near schools and medical services, many Bedouins camp near towns.

In an oasis village, people take advantage of the water supply to raise grain, fruit trees, and other crops. Their homes are made of stone or sun-dried mud. In these one- or two-story homes, farm animals often share the main floor.

The village well is a great meeting place for both villagers and Bedouin. Since everyone gathers at the well, it's only natural that souqs have grown up around them. In many villages, a mosque stands not far from the souq.

A camel gets a ride in the back of a pickup.

How the Islamic Calendar Works

The Islamic calendar is a lunar calendar. That means that the months follow the cycles of the moon, with each month lasting 29 or 30 days. Following the lunar cycles is considered a divine command, laid out in the Qur'an. Islamic astronomers determine the first day of each month by the rising of the new moon. In different parts of the world, the first day may differ because viewers see the moon rising at different times.

There are twelve months in a year, for a total of 354 days (355 days in leap years). That's eleven days shorter than the Western or Gregorian calendar, which is based on the solar (sun) year. As a result, Islamic religious holidays fall about eleven days earlier each year, according to the Western calendar. A centennial, or 100-year anniversary, is celebrated after ninety-seven years by the Western calendar.

"Year 1" for Muslims is A.D. 622—the year of the Prophet Muhammad's Hegira, or flight from Mecca to Medina. Year numbers are preceded by the letters A.H., meaning *anno hegirae* (year of the Hegira). In Saudi Arabia and much of the Middle East, the first day of A.H. 1423 was March 15, 2002. A.H. 1424 begins on March 4, 2003. A.H. 1425 begins on February 22, 2004, and so on.

Men in traditional summer thwab

Only family members can see this woman in her elaborate dress.

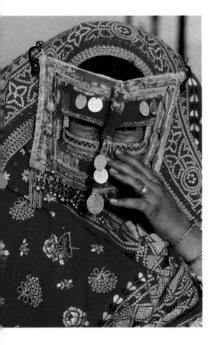

Clothing

The traditional clothing for both men and women in Saudi Arabia is long, loose, and flowing. It is ideal for the climate, where the heat can be relentless and winds often carry stinging sand. Because it covers most of the body, this clothing reflects Islamic ideals of modesty, too.

For a man, the traditional dress is the *thwab*—a long wool or cotton robe. The summer thwab is white, while the winter robe is dark. Over it, one wears a long cloak called a *bisht*. Made of sheep's wool or camel hair, the bisht is usually black, beige, or brown with gold edging. A man's traditional head-cloth is a *ghutra*. Made of cotton, the *ghutra* may be red-and-white checked or pure white. The coiled cord that holds it in place is an *igaal*. Underneath his headcloth, a man usually wears a skullcap, or *takiah*.

In the privacy of her home, a woman might wear a brightly colored dress with elaborate ornaments and jewelry. Traditional clothing styles vary from one region to another. In the Abha region, for example, women wear brightly colored dresses with beautiful embroidery, silver jewelry, and wide-brimmed straw hats. Some Saudi women may even wear high-fashion Western clothes at home. Only family and close friends will see this finery, though. In public, a woman wears an *abaya*—a long, black cloak that covers all her other clothing.

The variety of women's head scarves reflects different tastes and different degrees of modesty. Some women wear the *shayla tarha*, a scarf that covers only the hair. Others wear a *niqab*, a scarf with a veil over the face that reveals only

Life in the Compound

Many foreign businesspeople and their families live in compounds. Riyadh, Jiddah, and Dhahran are the main cities that host foreigners. Many foreigners work in the diplomatic corps in Riyadh. Jiddah is a commercial center, and the main business in the Gulf coast cities is oil.

Dhahran is called "the city that Aramco built." It consists almost entirely of a compound for Aramco employees from Western countries. The compound is fenced in, with security guards at every gate. Inside are schools, a library, a theater, a bowling alley, and a golf course. Families live in quiet, well-kept neighborhoods. Women are allowed to drive in the compound—a forbidden luxury outside its gates.

---

the eyes. The most modest is the *gholwa*, with a veil that covers the face completely.

Foreigners in Saudi Arabia are expected to dress modestly, too. For instance, a man may not wear shorts or go without a shirt in public. Women are expected to wear long skirts and long sleeves and to cover their hair. Even then, a woman in Western dress may be heckled or scolded. Her safest bet is simply to wear an abaya.

Women in Saudi Society

The subject of women has become a battleground for conservative and liberal forces in Saudi Arabia. More conservative Muslims believe that women should be completely separated from men in public life. They believe that a woman's education should cover only the skills she needs to take care of her home and family. Their rationale is that the family is the heart and core of Saudi society. A woman who takes care of her family without outside distractions and temptations is both a virtuous Muslim and an honorable member of her family

Women at work at King Abd al-Aziz University Hospital

Marriage, Saudi Style

Marriage in Saudi Arabia is a legal agreement rather than a religious vow. The marriage contract spells out the amount of money the husband must pay to the wife as a dowry, or wedding gift. After the couple and their witnesses sign the contract and the dowry is paid, the marriage is final.

and her society. More liberal Saudis believe that women should be free to take advantage of education and job opportunities. They favor modesty in women's dress rather than a complete cover-up.

From a Western point of view, Saudi women may seem oppressed. They must wear the abaya in public, and their movements outside the home are limited. To travel, a Saudi woman must have a male relative's written permission. She may not drive a car or attend sports events. However, many Saudi women are quick to point out the many freedoms they do enjoy and the legal rights they have.

A Saudi woman may sue her husband for divorce, for example. She has the right to own and inherit her own property. She also has the right to earn a university education. Women in Saudi Arabia work outside the home as nurses, teachers, and engineers, and in many other professions. Most working women are employed in all-female environments, such as women's hospital wards, girls' schools, and women's banks and stores. Women's education has advanced in Saudi Arabia faster than their job opportunities, however. There are now more qualified female college graduates in Saudi Arabia than there are jobs open to women.

Saudi women do not change their names after they marry, as many Western women do. Regardless of their marriage ties, they still belong to their father's ancestral family. Children take their father's last name. Married women are addressed as *Sayedah* ("Mrs."), while unmarried women are called *Aanisah* ("Miss").

The Hunter

Saudi children have played this traditional tag game for many generations. One player is chosen to be the hunter. With eyes closed, he or she counts to ten while the others run and hide. Then the hunter starts looking. Whoever is found starts running, while the hunter tries to tag the runner. If the hunter catches everyone, then the first person caught becomes the new hunter. Otherwise, the game begins again with the same person as the hunter.

Social Graces and Family Values

Hospitality is a tradition of desert dwellers. Since no one could survive alone in the desert, visitors were always welcomed with generous offerings of water, food, and shelter. Modern Saudis continue this tradition. They treat guests with genuine warmth and go out of their way to make sure they are comfortable and well-fed.

When Saudis meet for a social gathering, they are first served *qahweh* (Arabic coffee) and *shai* (sweet tea). Many people show their hospitality and respect for guests by burning incense. *Oud* (sandalwood) incense is the most prized.

When two men greet each other, they shake hands as they say, *"Assalaamu alaikum"* ("Peace be unto you"). The response is *"Wa-alaikum assalaam"* ("And unto you be peace"). Often they will also place their left hand on the other man's right shoulder and kiss him on both cheeks. In business dealings, it's not considered polite to get straight to the point. Instead, people are expected to spend some time in pleasant conversation and only gradually get around to the business at hand.

Qahweh being served

Living from Day to Day **123**

Saudi Scouts

Saudi boys can take part in scout programs through their schools. Like scouts in the United States, they move up through several ranks—Cubs, Scouts, Seniors, and Rovers. At each level, they work to earn merit badges for sports, nature, and community-service projects. Some of their community activities involve campaigning against drugs, encouraging safe driving, and cleaning up the environment. The most important volunteer work for many scouts is helping pilgrims on hajj to have a safe and comfortable visit. Although their activities may differ, they join scouts around the world in their commitment to honor God, country, and humanity.

Family is an important tradition in Saudi culture. The father is the authority in his immediate family, and the oldest male among a group of relatives is highly respected. Saudis are also very loyal to their clan, consisting of cousins and other extended family members, and to their tribe, which is made up of many clans. In fact, these family loyalties are stronger than political ties.

More Precious Than Gold

Since ancient times, merchants have collected rare incense from southern Arabia and southeast Asia. They carried their precious cargo on camel caravans along the ancient spice routes across deserts and mountain ranges. It was destined for markets in the Middle East, Africa, and Europe.

Today, oud (sandalwood) incense is more expensive than gold. It comes from the wood of the oud tree, which grows in only a few places in Asia. The finest, most fragrant oud incense comes from trees that have been infected with a certain bacteria for about 300 years. Many Saudi families burn oud as part of the celebrations at the end of Ramadan. Saudis buy almost 500 tons of oud incense every year.

Jasmine, amber, frankincense, and myrrh are some other precious incense substances. Frankincense and myrrh come from the southern part of the Arabian Peninsula. Ancient Greeks and Romans used them to treat illnesses. They were either applied as an ointment or burned while the patient inhaled the smoke.

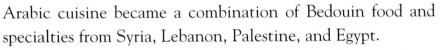
Food

Arabic food has its roots in the lifestyle of the Bedouins. They favored foods that could be carried easily, such as rice or dates, and food that could "travel," such as sheep and goats. Caravans passing through the Middle East introduced spices and vegetables from other lands. In time, Arabic cuisine became a combination of Bedouin food and specialties from Syria, Lebanon, Palestine, and Egypt.

The main foods in Saudi Arabia are lamb, dairy products, dates, and rice. Tea and coffee are the most popular drinks. Islamic law forbids eating pork and drinking alcoholic beverages. City residents and farmers also eat a variety of fruits and vegetables. Fast food is just as popular in Saudi Arabia as it is in the West. There are national Saudi fast-food chains, as well as McDonald's, Kentucky Fried Chicken, and Pizza Hut.

Khubz is a flat, round Arabic bread that can be split open and filled with meat or vegetables to make a sandwich. Khubz is sometimes torn apart to use for dipping or scooping up food. An important point of Arabic table manners is that only the right hand is used to bring food to the mouth.

Lunch is the main meal of the day. It's usually *kultra* (meat on skewers) or *kebabs*

Preparing traditional bread

Eating with the right hand is both customary and proper.

Food Vocabulary

qahweh	coffee
shai	tea
ma'a	water
haleeb	milk
khubz	bread
sokar	sugar
melh	salt

(meatballs) with soup and vegetables. Other favorite foods are grilled chicken, *felafel* (deep-fried balls of mashed fava beans), *shwarma* (sliced lamb cooked on a spit), and *fuul* (fava beans mashed with garlic and lemon).

Qahweh—Arabic coffee—is a dark and fragrant drink. It's a mixture of unroasted coffee beans and cardamom pods. Served in small cups, qahweh is meant to be sipped slowly. *Shai* is a sweet tea, served in small glasses, often with mint flavoring added. Fresh milk in Saudi Arabia comes from cows, camels, sheep, and goats. Nomads also developed many dairy products by fermenting milk in animal-hide bags. *Laban* is a drinkable yogurt similar to buttermilk, while *zabadi* is set yogurt. *Labneh* is cream cheese, also known as *fromage frais* (French for "fresh cheese"). *Ghista* is a spoonable cream. Saudis also enjoy European-style yogurts and *zady*, a *laban* with fruit.

For Bedouins, camel milk and coffee are the main beverages. The main meal is eaten in the evening. A typical meal consists of *kapsa* (a lamb and rice dish) and *acida* (balls of dough dipped in melted butter). Food is served in platters on small wooden stands, and everyone gathers around to share.

Special Days and Times

Saudis celebrate two special religious holidays every year. Eid al-Fitr is the feast that celebrates the breaking of the fast. It begins on the twenty-fifth day of Ramadan and lasts until the fifth of the next month. Eid al-Adha celebrates the end of the hajj. It lasts from the fifth through the fifteenth of Dhu al-Hijjah, the twelfth month.

Khubz (Arabic Bread)

Ingredients:

2 teaspoons dry yeast

1 cup warm water

3 cups flour

1 teaspoon salt

Directions:

Dissolve the yeast in the warm water. Sift together the flour and salt, then mix in the yeast and water. Turn out the mixture onto a floured surface and knead it for several minutes. Form the dough into a ball, put it in a deep bowl, cover it with a damp cloth, and let it rise in a warm place for about 3 hours.

Preheat the oven to 350°F. Divide the dough into six equal parts and roll them into balls. Press or roll each ball into a circle about one-half-inch thick. Place them on an ungreased baking sheet and bake for 10 minutes or until they are golden-brown.

Cut a bread circle in half and fill it with meat or vegetables to make a sandwich. For dipping, cut each circle into wedges.

For leisure time and vacations, many Saudis go to the beaches on the Red Sea coast or the Gulf coast south of Dammam. The scenic Asir Mountains in the southwest and the lush resort of Ta'if, in the Hijaz east of Jeddah, are popular spots, too.

Friday is the day of prayer and rest for Muslims, as Sunday is for Christians and Saturday is for Jews. The Muslim work-week begins on Saturday and lasts through Thursday. Government offices and many other businesses are closed on Thursdays. So the "weekend," corresponding to Saturday and Sunday in the West, is Thursday and Friday.

Shops are usually open from about 9:30 A.M. to 2:00 P.M. and 5:00 P.M. to 10:00 P.M., closing for the hottest part of the afternoon. But all shops close for about 30 minutes at prayer times. No matter how important their business matters are—no matter how much money or honor is at stake—Saudis remember life's priorities. Their first loyalty is to the one they address in prayer: "Allah, the Most Gracious, the Most Merciful."

Timeline

Saudi Arabian History

Muhammad al-Sa'ud joins Muhammad bin Abd al-Wahhab in holy war.	1806
The Sa'ud family is forced from Saudi Arabia by the Rashids.	1891
Abd al-Aziz bin Abd ar-Rahman bin Faisal al-Sa'ud begins a campaign to regain control of Saudi Arabia.	1902
Abd al-Aziz founds kingdom of Saudi Arabia.	1932
Oil is discovered in Saudi Arabia.	1933
American oil companies drilling in Saudi Arabia form Aramco.	1944
King Faisal brings about economic and social reforms.	1964–1975
Organization of Petroleum Exporting Countries (OPEC), including Saudi Arabia, imposes an oil embargo on Western nations, including the United States.	1973
King Khalid uses profits from oil to improve cities, roads, and airports.	1975–1982
In the Persian Gulf War, Saudi Arabia is part of a coalition that attacks Iraq for seizing Kuwait.	1990–1991
King Fahd sets up a Consultative Council.	1992
A terrorist attack kills U.S. soldiers near Dhahran.	1996
Saudi Arabia wins its first medal in the Olympic Games in Sydney, Australia.	2000

World History

1776	The Declaration of Independence is signed.
1789	The French Revolution begins.
1865	The American Civil War ends.
1914	World War I breaks out.
1917	The Bolshevik Revolution brings communism to Russia.
1929	Worldwide economic depression begins.
1939	World War II begins, following the German invasion of Poland.
1945	World War II ends.
1957	The Vietnam War starts.
1969	Humans land on the moon.
1975	The Vietnam War ends.
1979	Soviet Union invades Afghanistan.
1983	Drought and famine in Africa.
1989	The Berlin Wall is torn down, as communism crumbles in Eastern Europe.
1991	Soviet Union breaks into separate states.
1992	Bill Clinton is elected U.S. president.
2000	George W. Bush is elected U.S. president.

Fast Facts

Official name: Kingdom of Saudi Arabia

Capital: Riyadh

Official language: Arabic

Old homes in a Jiddah alley

Saudi Arabia's flag

The Najd

Official religion:	Islam
Year of founding:	1932
Founder:	King Abd al-Aziz bin Abd ar-Rahman bin Faisal al-Sa'ud
National anthem:	*"Sarei lil majd walaya"* ("Onward Towards the Glory and the Heights")
Government:	Monarchy
Chief of state:	King
Area:	830,000 square miles (2,149,690 sq km)
Dimensions:	East/West, 1,290 miles (2,076 km) North/South, 1,145 miles (1,843 km)
Latitude and longitude of geographic center:	25° North, 45° East
Borders:	Jordan, Iraq, and Kuwait to the north; the Persian Gulf, Qatar, and the United Arab Emirates to the east; Oman and Yemen to the south; the Red Sea to the west; the Gulf of Aqaba to the northwest
Highest elevation:	Jabal Sawda, 10,279 feet (3,133 m) above sea level
Lowest elevation:	Sea level along the Persian Gulf
Average temperature:	32°F (0°C) in January; 120°F (49°C) in July
Average annual rainfall:	0 inches in the Rub' al-Khali; 20 inches (51 cm) in the Asir region
National population (2000 est.):	22,246,000

Nabataen City entrance

Population of largest cities (1995 est):

Riyadh	2,620,000
Jiddah	1,500,000
Mecca	770,000
Medina (1992)	608,300
Ta'if (1992)	416,100

Famous landmarks:

- ▶ *Aramco Exhibit/Museum*, Dhahran
- ▶ *Asir National Park*, southwestern Saudi Arabia
- ▶ *Dir'aiyah ruins*, north of Riyadh
- ▶ *Jubbah rock drawings*, Nafud desert
- ▶ *Mada'in Salah rock tombs*, northwest of Medina
- ▶ *Mahazat as-Sayd Protected Area*, near Ta'if
- ▶ *Masmak Fortress*, Riyadh
- ▶ *Mosque of the Prophet*, Medina
- ▶ *Museum of Abdel Raouf Hasan Khali*, Jiddah
- ▶ *Holy Mosque and Ka'abah*, Mecca
- ▶ *Shuhbra Palace*, Ta'if
- ▶ *Souq al-Alawi*, Jiddah

Industry: Saudi Arabia's economy is based on petroleum. It has the world's largest reserves of petroleum and is the world's largest exporter of petroleum. Saudi Arabia is also a leading producer of natural gas. In recent years, the government has encouraged the development of other industries that make products such as chemicals, fertilizer, and steel.

Currency: The Saudi *riyal* (SR) is the basic monetary unit. In May 2002, U.S. $1 equaled 3.75 SR

System of weights and measures: Metric system

Literacy (1999): 90 percent (men)
70 percent (women)

Currency

Herder with his goats

King Faud

Common words and phrases:

marahaba (mar-HA-ba)	hi/hello
Massalama (MA- ëa s-sa-LEH-ma)	good-bye
sabah al-khair (sa-BAH il-KHEYR)	good morning
masah al-khair (mi-SEH il-KHEYR)	good evening
Kaif halak?/Kaif halik? (Keyf HEH-lak/keyf HEH-lik)	How are you? (to a man)/ (to a woman)
al-hamdu lillah (il-HAM-du lil-LEH)	fine
min fadlak/min fadlik (min FAD-lak/min FAD-lik)	please (to a man)/ (to a woman)
shukran (SHUK-ran)	thank you

Famous People:

Abd al-Aziz bin Abd ar-Rahman
bin Faisal al-Sa'ud   (1880–1953)
*Founder of the Kingdom of Saudi Arabia
and ruler of the kingdom until 1953*

Abdullah bin al-Aziz   (1942–)
Crown prince and future king of Saudi Arabia

Ahmad Zaki Yamani   (1930–)
Former Saudi minister of petroleum

Fahd bin Abd al-Aziz al-Sa'ud   (1923–)
Present king of Saudi Arabia

Faisal bin Abd al-Aziz al-Sa'ud   (1906–1975)
*Brought economic and social reforms to
Saudi Arabia during his reign (1964–1975)*

Hadi Souan Somayli   (1976–)
First athlete to win an Olympic medal for Saudi Arabia

Muhammad   (570–632)
Founder of Islam

Muhammad bin Abd al-Wahhab   (1703–1792)
Reformer who urged strict observance of Islamic laws

To Find Out More

Nonfiction

▶ Anderson, Laurie Halse and Helga Jones. *Saudi Arabia* (Globe-Trotters Club). Minneapolis: Carolrhoda, 2000.

▶ Goodwin, William. *Saudi Arabia* (Modern Nations of the World). Farmington Hills, MI: Lucent Books, 2001.

▶ Honeyman, Susan. *Saudi Arabia* (Country Fact Files). Austin, TX: Raintree/Steck-Vaughn, 1995.

▶ Janin, Hunt. *Saudi Arabia* (Cultures of the World). Tarrytown, NY: Benchmark Books, 1995.

▶ Mulloy, Martin. *Saudi Arabia* (Major World Nations). New York, NY: Chelsea House, 1998.

▶ O'Shea, Maria. *Saudi Arabia* (Festivals of the World). Milwaukee: Gareth Stevens, 1999.

▶ Tames, Richard and Sheila. *Muslim* (Beliefs and Cultures series). Danbury, CT: Children's Press, 1996.

▶ Temple, Bob. *Saudi Arabia* (Countries: Faces and Places). Chanhassen, MN: Child's World, 2000.

Videotapes

▶ *Ancient Arabia.* World Almanac Video, 1999.

▶ *National Geographic's Arabia: Sand, Sea and Sky.* National Geographic, 1998.

▶ *Saudi Arabia.* Three-video series, 59 minutes each. San Francisco State University, 1982.

Websites

▶ **Royal Embassy of Saudi Arabia**
http://www.saudiembassy.net
Information on Saudi Arabia's geography, economy, culture, archaeological sites, and more.

▶ **Arabian Adventures**
http://www.kfshrc.edu.sa/arabian/index.html
An exploration of Saudi Arabia's culture, religion, customs, daily life, and many other subjects.

▶ **Arabian Wildlife**
http://www.arabianwildlife.com/main.htm
Fascinating articles about the animals and plants of Saudi Arabia.

Embassy

▶ **Royal Embassy of Saudi Arabia**
601 New Hampshire Ave., NW
Washington, DC 20037
1-202-337-4076

Index

Page numbers in *italics* indicate illustrations.

Shi'ite Muslims, 22, 48, 96
spread of, *48*
Sunnah (traditions), 49, 98
Sunni Muslims, 48, 96

J

Jabal Sawda, 18, 20
Jabal Tuwayq, 21
jasmine, 39
Jenadriyah Heritage and Cultural
    Festival, 110
jerboas, 31, *31*
jewelry, 105, *105*
Jiddah, *10*, 19, 27, 62, 85–86, 87, 99,
    110, *110*, 111, 121
Jubail, 22, 74, 82
Jubbah, 29
judicial system
    Court of Cassation, 65
    General Courts, 65
    Mutawa'een ("religious police"),
        67, *67*
    punishments, 66, *66*
    Summary Courts, 65
    Supreme Court of Justice, 65

K

Ka'abah (shrine), 46, 101, *101*, 103
kauf (storm), 26
Khafaji, Ibrahim, 62
Khalid (kind), 55
al-Khobar, 21–22, 27
khubz (bread), 125, *125*, 127
al-Khwarazmi (mathematician), 107
Kindah (Bedouin kingdom), 43
Kindite culture, 43
King Abd al-Aziz Historical
    Center, 111
King Abd al-Aziz International
    Airport, 81

King Abd al-Aziz Library and
    Auditorium, 111
King Abd al-Aziz University
    Hospital, *122*
King Fahd International Airport, 81
King Fahd Stadium, 112, 114, *114*
King Fahd University of Petroleum
    and Minerals, 22
King Faud Causeway, 81
King Khalid International Airport,
    81, *81*
King Sa'ud University, 93, *93*
kings, 54–55, *55*, 57, 59–60
King's Camel Race, 112, *112*
Koran. *See* Qur'an.

L

Lakhmid Bedouin culture, 42–43
language, 13, 89–90, *91*, 98, 106–107
    calligraphy, 91, 105, 106
    Gulf dialect, 90
    Hijazi dialect, 90
    Najdi dialect, 90
    numerals, 107
    writing system, 90–91
Lawrence, T. E., 53, *53*
literature, 107, 108, *108*
local government.
    See also government.
    General Administration
        Committee, 63
    General Municipal Councils, 62–63
    governing councils, 63, *63*
    governors, 62
    Minister of the Interior, 62
    provinces, 62, *63*
locusts, 36

M

Mada'in Saleh, 42, 43, *43*
Mahazat as-Sayd, 29

Mahd al-Dhahab gold mine, 76
Majlis as-Shura (Consultative
    Council), 57, 61, *61*
manufacturing, 72, 74, *75*
maps. *See also* historical maps.
    geopolitical, *12*
    natural resources, *74*
    oilfields, *71*
    population density, *85*
    provinces, *63*
    regions, *63*
    Riyadh, *64*
    topographical, *18*
marine life, 31–32, *31*
marriage, *122*
Masmak Fortress, 111
Mecca, 11, *11*, 27, 44, *44*, 45, 46, 49,
    53, 57, 62, 85–86, 87, 96, 100,
    101, 103
medical care, 88
Medina, 11, 17, 27, 45, *45*, 46, 49,
    57, 62, 85–86, 87, 96, 101, *101*
Middle East, 15
military, 84
Mina, 103
Minaean culture, 42
mining, 72, 74, 76, *76*
monsoons, 25
Mosque of Mohammad bin Abd
    al-Wahhab, 51
Mosque of the Prophet Muhammad,
    27, 101, *101*
mosques, 27, 51, 95, 99–100, *99*, 101,
    101, 111
mountains, 18, 20, 21
Muhammad (prophet), 11, 27, 44–46,
    59, 96, 97
music, 108–109, *109*
al-Mutanabbi (poet), 107
Mutawa'een ("religious police"), 67, *67*
myrrh, 124

Meet the Author

Ann Heinrichs fell in love with faraway places while reading Doctor Dolittle books as a child. Now she tries to cover as much of the Earth as possible. She has traveled through most of the United States and much of Europe, as well as the Middle East, East Asia, and Africa. Her time in Egypt, Jordan, and West Africa provided a world of insights into—and appreciation of—Arab and Islamic cultures.

Ann grew up roaming the woods of Arkansas. Now she lives in Chicago. She is the author of more than seventy books for children and young adults on American, European, Asian, and African history and culture.

"To me, writing nonfiction is a bigger challenge than writing fiction. With nonfiction, you can't just dream something up—everything has to be true. Finding out facts is harder than making things up, but to me it's more rewarding. When I uncover the facts, they always turn out to be more spectacular than fiction could ever be."

Two of Ann's Children's Press books—*Australia*, in the Enchantment of the World series, and *Louisa Catherine Johnson Adams*, in the Encyclopedia of First Ladies series—were national first-place award–winners in the National Federation of Press Women's communications competition. Several of her other books have won national and state awards as well.

She has also written numerous newspaper, magazine, and encyclopedia articles. As an advertising copywriter, she has covered everything from plumbing hardware to Oriental rugs. She holds bachelor's and master's degrees in piano performance. These days, however, her performing arts are t'ai chi empty-hand and sword forms. She is an award-winning martial artist and participates in regional and national tournaments.

Photo Credits

Photographs © 2002:

AP/Wide World Photos: 60 (Kamran Jebreili), 55, 133 bottom (Tannen Maury), 114 top (Dimitri Messinis), 122 (Juwayriya Paxton), 82 bottom (Mariam Sami), 72 (Ronald Zak), 58;
Archive Photos/Getty Images: 53;
Art Resource, NY: 7 bottom, 41 (Erich Lessing), 44;
Bridgeman Art Library International Ltd., London/New York: 108 top (Victoria & Albert Museum, London, UK, "The Arabian Nights", by Edmund Dulac, reproduced by permission of Hodder and Stoughton Limited), 40 (Whitford & Hughes, London, UK), 49 (British Museum, London, UK), 45 (Chester Beatty Library, Dublin);
Byron Augustin: 10 bottom, 36, 51, 81, 87, 91, 93, 98, 109, 114 bottom;
Corbis Images/Reuters NewMedia Inc.: 115;
Envision/Moshe Zur: 38;
Hulton Archive/Getty Images: 54;
Magnum Photos: 56, 101 right (Abbas), 76, 80 bottom, 95 (Marc Riboud), cover, 6, 88 bottom, 118 (George Rodger);
NASA: 15;
National Geographic Image Collection: 124 (Thomas J. Abercrombie), 113 (Jodi Cobb);
Peter Arnold Inc.: 30, 31 center, 33 top (X. Eichaker/Bios), 35 (M. Gunther/Bios), 69 (Robert Mackinlay);

Photo Researchers, NY: 11, 27, 106 (Mehmet Biber), 20 top (C.J. Collins), 7 top, 10 top, 16 bottom, 24, 79, 117, 125 top, 131 bottom (Ray Ellis), 123 (Rick Golt), 9 (Allen Green), 110, 130 left (Hubertus Kanus), 120 bottom (Thierry Mauger), 29, 31 top (Tom McHugh), 105, 116 (Visuals Departures, LTD.);
Rebecca Augustin: 67;
Stone/Getty Images: 92, 112, 125 bottom (Wayne Eastep), 2, 101 left (Nabeel Turner);
The Image Works: 94 (Bill Gallery), 77 (John Moore), 88 top (Tony O'Brien);
TRIP Photo Library: 47 (M. Good), 99 (OP), 31 bottom (M. Portelly), 26, 28, 42 (H. Rogers), 14, 19, 23, 39, 43, 64 left, 66, 73, 75 top, 75 bottom, 78, 80 top, 84, 103, 104, 132 top, 132 bottom, 133 top;
Visuals Unlimited: 33 bottom (Gerald & Buff Corsi), 37 (Barbra Hesse), 32 (Ken Lucas);
Woodfin Camp & Associates: 8, 82 top, 108 bottom, 119, 120 top (Robert Azzi), 16 top (Tony Howarth), 63 bottom, 86 (Barry Iverson), 70 (Tom Stoddart/Katz), 100 (William Strode).

Maps by Joe LeMonnier